"My Goodness — My Guinness"

G.E.1130

September 1939: how to deal with a possible gas attack – oilskins and a respirator for the man, sacking to protect the eyes, nose and mouth of the horse.

Title page: harrowing in Wales in October 1940.

WAR IN THE COUNTRYSIDE
1939-45
Sadie Ward

WILTSHIRE
COUNTY COUNCIL
LIBRARY &
MUSEUM SERVICE

CAMERON BOOKS
in association with
DAVID & CHARLES

Published by Cameron Books,
2a Roman Way, London N7 8XG
in association with David & Charles Publishers plc
Brunel House, Newton Abbot, Devon TQ12 4PU
Distributed by David & Charles Publishers plc

Edited and designed by Ian Cameron

Reproduction by B.B. Associates, Chichester
Printed by Eastern Press, Reading

Printed and bound in Great Britain

ISBN 0 7153 9295 6

The majority of the illustrations in this book are from the
collection of the Institute of Agricultural History and
Museum of English Rural Life, University of Reading.
Other illustrations appear by permission of the following:

BBC Hulton Pictury Library 84, 86a, 86c, 87a, 91, 93, 95,
    100, 101, 184
Imperial War Museum 39a, 39c, 40b, 43a, 85a, 85b, 86b,
    88, 89a, 89b, 96a, 96b, 97, 98a, 98b, 99, 104b, 119, 146,
    158
Keystone Collection 16, 46, 47b, 74, 82, 85b, 87b, 110,
    116, 130, 133b, 134a, 134b, 139, 140, 141, 142, 143
Popperfoto 126, 128, 149
Suffolk Record Office 83
Topham Picture Library 76, 108, 135, 136, 137, 138

The David Low cartoon on p.35 is reproduced by courtesy
of the London *Evening Standard*.

I am particularly grateful to the following, who kindly sent
me their reminiscences of the war years, from which I have
quoted in the text.

H.E. Bell, Reading, Berkshire
Marjorie Blackmore, Bridlington, East Yorkshire
Joyce Burton, High Wycombe, Buckinghamshire
Marjorie Byers, St Albans, Hertfordshire
B.A.N. Green, Sands, Farnham, Surrey
T.B. Hartman, Thurlbear, Taunton, Somerset
Peter Hollis, Sudbury, Suffolk
B.N. Jackson, Haslingfield, Cambridge
Sylvia Knight, York
C. Maddocks, Whixall, Whitchurch, Shropshire
I. McWilliam, Ravenglass, Cumbria
'S.P.', Berkhamsted, Hertfordshire
J. Pickard, Ramsey, Huntingdonshire
S. Pratt, Twyford, Reading, Berkshire
D. Shirra, Longden, Shrewsbury, Shropshire
Mrs Hugh Taylor, Cricket St Thomas, Chard, Somerset

I would also like to thank Mrs L. Delaney of the
Farmland Museum, Haddenham, Cambridgeshire for
sending me extracts from her aunt's diary and David St
John Thomas for recording his wartime reminiscences of
rural Devon on tape and making this available to me.

In addition I have received much valuable advice from
C.S. Smith of Slough, Berkshire, a leading journalist with
The Farmers Weekly for many years. I have used a number
of Mr Smith's comments on the interwar period in the
Introduction. I have benefited, too, from the many
informative conversations I have had with Bill Petch of
Woodley, Reading, Berkshire, who was a farm worker in
Huntingdonshire during the Second World War.

Finally, I wish to express my appreciation of the help
and encouragement given by Ian Cameron and Jill Hollis
of Cameron Books throughout this project. I owe further
thanks to Christine Chodun for keying my manuscript
directly into a computer, undertaken with much efficiency
and good humour.

In writing this book, one of the best and as yet unused
sources has proved to be the farming press. I have,
therefore, drawn extensively on two publications of
consistently high quality, namely *The Farmers Weekly* and
The Farmer & Stock-breeder. I have also found *Country
Life* and *The Field* good sources of interesting information
and anecdotes on wider aspects of country life between
1939 and 1945.

A helpful and well-illustrated introduction to this
subject is Ian Grant and Nicholas Maddren, *The
Countryside at War* (Jupiter Books, 1975). I am obliged to
both authors for a number of facts, relating especially to
the Home Guard and evacuees.

Beyond this I made considerable use of two important
reference works. The first is Keith Murray's official study,
History of the Second World War: Agriculture (H.M.S.O.
and Longman, Green and Co, 1955), which provided
many of the statistics and related data used in the
Introduction and Chapter 1. The second is that by R.J.
Hammond, *Food and Agriculture in Britain 1939-1945:
Aspects of Wartime Control* (Stanford University Press
1954). This is an excellent guide to the complexities of
Government food policy, from which I have extracted
details of the various rationing schemes. Both Murray and
Hammond are now dated in some respects, but there has
not yet been any serious academic treatise to replace them.
Comments on Government agricultural policy during the
First World War and for the period after 1945 have partly
been taken from the excellent historical survey by Michael
Tracy, *Agriculture in Western Europe: Challenge and
Response 1880-1980* (Granada, 2nd edition, 1982).

Other works consulted are mentioned, where
appropriate, in the main body of the text.

For my mother Kathleen Betty (Lowman) Ward
and in memory of my father John Kingdon Ward

CONTENTS

Chapter 1
MOBILISING THE LAND

Sunday, 3rd September 1939, started gloriously. The sun was breaking through the morning mist as people filed into church, but when the congregations emerged the news went round that Britain was at war again. There was little shock or surprise, only a grim determination in the countryside, as in the towns and cities, to put things right once and for all. On a Wiltshire lane, A.G. Street met an eighty-year-old farm labourer who was already carrying a gas mask slung over his shoulder. The old man had never thought it would come to this, but things couldn't go on as they had for the past year or two – old Hitler's comb, he said, must be cut.

Country people were ready to do all that was expected of them, and more, but meanwhile they tried to carry on as usual. Within a day or two of the declaration of war, the Barnstaple Fair authorities in Devon had resolved to go ahead with their traditional toast and ale ceremony and to maintain the continuity of a fair that had been established more than a thousand years before by King Aethelstan. To have panicked and cancelled the event, they decided, was not the English way. People up and down the country were showing in a thousand ways that it would take more than a state of war to budge them from their normal routine.

Already, though, there were signs of unusual activity. At Boscombe, in Leicestershire, the entire football team turned out to help with the harvest before, as they said, the sirens sounded across the farmyard. From Staffordshire came news that Salt and Saucy, two elephants from John Swallow's circus, were being tried out for work of national importance, providing extra power for the autumn ploughing.

The first official steps to put Britain's farms on a war footing were taken in the last days of peacetime, at the end of August, although the process by which the government took control of the land went back to the mid-'thirties, when the Ministry of Agriculture began to consider how food could be a decisive factor in a war against Germany. Even so, Britain started the war at a great disadvantage: after Hitler came to power in 1933, Germany had striven to reduce its dependence on outside supplies, so that by 1939 it was more than four-fifths self-sufficient in food. In contrast, British farmers were managing to produce only thirty per cent of the nation's food requirements.

Memories coloured by nostalgia recall the British countryside in the years between the two world wars as being neatly quilted with a green patchwork of fields. In fact, it was one of the most dilapidated landscapes in western Europe. Agriculture was in a state of depression: many farmers had pulled out altogether, and those who remained were having to struggle to survive. Great swathes of land that had once been productive were reverting to waste.

British farming had been on the decline since the 1870s, a victim of Britain's commitment to free trade. The idea had been that the country's prosperity as an industrial nation was best served by exporting high-value manufactured products in return for cheap raw materials and food. Through the open door of free trade flooded such commodities as wheat, which could be grown much more cheaply on the virgin soils of North America than by efficient but expensive farming at home. With steam ships cutting the cost of transport across the Atlantic and refrigeration allowing meat as well as cereals to be imported cheaply, the golden age of British farming was at an end. The worst of the decline was over by the mid-1890s, but there was little sign of recovery before World War I. Although the anticipation of fewer imports made the price of wheat rise in 1914, most farmers were content to take the profits without investing in extra production. Doubtless they felt, like everyone else, that the war would last only a few months, and then the boom would be over. It was not until late in 1916 that a poor harvest and the German announcement of a policy of unrestricted submarine warfare made official intervention unavoidable. In December that year, a new coalition government under David Lloyd George took office and appointed a Food Controller. County Agricultural Executive Committees were set up, with powers to order the ploughing up of grassland and to take possession of badly run farms. Guaranteed minimum prices were introduced for cereals and potatoes, albeit at a level below the current market, but the principle of state support for farming had been established. In 1917 and 1918, one and three quarter million acres of grassland were ploughed up to grow wheat.

After the war, there was much debate as to whether the policy of government guarantees to sustain food production should be continued. In 1920, the Agriculture Act continued the support, but by 1921 world grain supplies had risen and prices had fallen sharply, making the cost of subsidies escalate. Fearing an open-ended commitment, the government hastily repealed the Agriculture Act and left the farmers to fend for themselves.

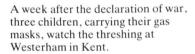

A week after the declaration of war, three children, carrying their gas masks, watch the threshing at Westerham in Kent.

Worse was yet to come with the beginning of the Great Depression in 1929, which affected town and country alike. Between 1929 and 1932, farm prices fell by over a third in an almost unprecedented slump. Farmers faced the future with a deep feeling of pessimism. In the twenty years between the wars, as much as a third of the labour force left the land as farmers changed to less intensive and less costly forms of agriculture.

Arable land was given over to grass, and vast areas of mainly marginal farmland simply became derelict. Fields that had become overgrown with weeds and scrub were a common sight on the Fetwold and Methwold Fens in East Anglia and across the 'three-horse' clays of Essex and the South Midlands. The cost of draining heavy soils became uneconomic, and they became waterlogged and rank, while hill farmers were no longer able to maintain enough livestock for the grazing to keep the pastures open. On acid soils, the liming that was needed to keep the bracken at bay was neglected, as was the burning of heather on the Scottish hills – if heather is left more than seven years, it becomes woody and will not regenerate when it is burnt. The result was serious erosion in mountain areas such as the Cairngorms. Everywhere the countryside was visibly impoverished, whether in the abandoned hill farms of mid-Wales or in the burgeoning hedgerows of the south of England where farmers could no longer afford to employ skilled hedgers – near Basingstoke in Hampshire, hedges reached 18 feet in height and spread so much that when one field was eventually ploughed and its hedge cut back, it grew from 20 acres to 22 acres.

Some farmers went broke and left farming altogether, some held on grimly, tightening their belts and spending as little as possible, but a few managed to do better, particularly in dairy farming, as there was a growing demand for milk, which was anyway a commodity that enjoyed natural protection from foreign competitors. The most astute, however, took advantage of cheap land values to buy or rent large acreages in the hope of future gain. By the early 1930s, farming was in sufficient distress that the Government had to take action. It reintroduced price support, created marketing boards to improve distribution, and negotiated import quotas with foreign suppliers, although the idea of Imperial Preference meant that supplies from the Empire still rose by nearly half between 1932 and 1939. At the outbreak of war, some seventy per cent of Britain's

To show that food imports are still arriving, W.S. Morrison, the Minister of Food, visits London Docks on 5th December 1939 and watches mutton being unloaded.

A traditional scene: carting wheatsheaves in Berkshire.

requirements for food and livestock feeding stuffs were being imported, leaving the country extremely vulnerable to blockade.

Almost to the end of the 'thirties, successive Cabinets could see no reasons on defence grounds for doing anything about the state of British agriculture. Should war break out, they thought, there would be time to inaugurate a ploughing-up campaign and use the reserves of fertility that had been put into the soil from the dung of livestock that had been fattened on cheap imported feed. Nevertheless, in 1935, Walter Elliot, the Minister of Agriculture, set up a committee to look at the way farming should be organised in wartime. Its recommendations for proper government planning and the reconstitution of the County Agricultural Committees that had done much sterling work during the Great War were taken up by the Imperial Defence Sub-Committee on Food Supply in Time of War, which was formed after Hitler's illegal occupation of the Rhineland in March 1936. By the end of that year, there was a scheme for the establishment of a committee in every county, with a chairman, executive officer and secretary provisionally selected for each, although the people nominated remained unaware of their coming importance in the County Agricultural Committees, which would become generally known as War Ags.

The government's feeling that it needed to do nothing beyond improving the condition of the land was reflected in the Agricultural Act of 1937 which offered grants to farmers to buy lime and basic slag and to invest in the drainage of their land. By the spring of 1939, the Germans had been occupying Austria for more than a year and were pushing out from Sudetenland (which they had been granted by the Munich conference the previous autumn) to take over much of Czechoslovakia. It was only at this point that the British Government came to realise that the country lacked any perceptible reserves of fertilisers, feeding stuffs and agricultural machinery, although the need to stockpile these had been accepted since 1936. Accordingly, the new Minister of Agriculture, Sir Reginald Dorman-Smith, went

August 1939 in North Devon: sheep block a lane on their way to new pastures on Exmoor.

on a buying spree for phosphate rock, oil seeds, cereal feeding stuffs and tractors – some 3,000 to 5,000 of them with their associated implements, to be acquired from British and American manufacturers. Farmers were offered a payment of £2 for every acre of permanent grassland ploughed up between 3rd May and 30th September 1939. Financial incentives were offered for growing barley and oats to replace imported animal feed. To stop a wartime ploughing-up campaign being frustrated by shortage of labour, the age at which tractor drivers and other agricultural mechanics qualified as being exempt from conscription was lowered from 25 to 21.

All this frenetic eleventh-hour activity was paralleled by similar last-minute efforts by the government on the food control front. Back in 1936, a committee under Sir William Beveridge (Director of the London School of Economics) had pointed out the need for a whole system of food requisition and distribution. Accordingly, the government set up a Food (Defence Plans) Department, but, by the time of Munich, very little had happened: not a single commodity control scheme was ready and no ration books had been printed. Thereafter, the pace quickened, and the chronically understaffed Department was enlarged to become the nucleus of a wartime Ministry of Food. Security stocks of food were built up and, during the course of 1939, iron rations were reserved for the several million people scheduled to be evacuated from London and the other threatened cities.

At the end of August 1939, just before the outbreak of war, the government's food plans were put into effect. The Defence of the Realm Act gave the Minister of Agriculture complete authority to control and direct food production, including the right to take possession of any farm or to terminate any agricultural tenancy where the land was being neglected or badly cultivated. The War Ags, already formed, were put on stand-by and within a few days had been told to carry out their instructions 'as a matter of urgency'. The government announced that it was taking full powers to fix the prices of farm produce, and after Christmas 1939, it seized control of livestock: animals for slaughter now had to be sold to the state at a guaranteed price.

The first priority was to increase production of food crops by ploughing up permanent pasture – the eventual target was two million acres of newly ploughed arable land before the 1940 harvest. The ploughing up of pasture inevitably meant fewer animals, although the War Cabinet wanted to keep livestock production going as long as possible, not only to keep meat in the British diet but also to sustain the fertility of the soil, which depended on animal manure. In the event of a critical shortage of feeding stuffs, cattle and sheep would be given priority, and pig and poultry producers were warned that their animals might have to be slaughtered.

For growers whose crops were viewed as luxuries, the war was to involve particular sacrifice. The celebrated rose-grower Harry Wheatcroft recalled in 1942:

We put the plough through a field of some hundred thousand trees – a heartbreaking job. We tore from the greenhouses the bushes that were to give us blooms for the spring flower shows, and so made room for the more urgent bodily needs of the nation.

Pigs now wander about where our Polyantha roses bloomed. There's wheat and barley where acres of Hybrid Teas coloured the land – even the humble cabbage stands where standard roses once held majestic sway. The odour of our glasshouses has changed too. Here half a million onion plants have taken the place of the roses. They, in turn, will be succeeded by tomato plants and fruit; then lettuce, while the light still holds, and afterwards the humble mustard and cress . . .

All nurserymen in every county are making these drastic changes; much beauty has been destroyed and there's no need to pretend that it hasn't meant a heavy financial loss. Carnations, roses, flowering plants, trees and shrubs yield a good deal more in cash per acre than the crops and vegetables I've mentioned. However, our actions today can't be measured by money, and perhaps we should be proud that our business has found us in charge of a small piece of British soil that we can now use for the country's good.

Another flower grower, E. Watts of Devoran, near Truro in Cornwall, had already turned over much of his farm to vegetables and cereals by 1942 when he told wireless listeners:

Next week I'm hiring in a tractor to plough . . . under daffodil bulbs in fields which will be carrying a corn crop this summer, followed by cabbages next winter. Ploughing under these bulbs means a *tremendous* loss to me. We flower farmers have been a lifetime building up our stock of daffodils, and the bulbs represent much of

In an advertisement in *The Farmer & Stock-breeder*, the Ministry of Food reminds farmers that from 15th January 1940 it will be their only customer for livestock. The abattoir gates at Shrewsbury Market are opened for the first supply of Government cattle.

MINISTRY  OF FOOD

URGENT NOTICE TO
FARMERS

On and after Monday 15th January the Ministry of Food becomes the sole buyer, at fixed published prices, of all fatstock (including pigs) for slaughter. Farmers thus have a guaranteed market, but it is conditional upon their giving due notice of their intention to send stock to the markets or to the bacon factories.

PLOUGH NOW !

by day...

and night...

...AND BEAT THE WEATHER!

A Ministry of Agriculture advertisement in *The Farmers Weekly* of 15th March 1940 urges farmers to greater efforts. It adds: 'By ploughing now you can win the equivalent of a mighty naval battle! . . . Win *your* Graf Spee battle of production by ploughing up now!'

our capital. I've already ploughed out practically half what I had, and you can quite imagine how I feel towards this utter destruction. The bulbs have to lie out in heaps to rot. But that doesn't count much in war-time.

An excessively wet October and November preceded the first winter of the war. Frost and heavy snow in January followed by a bitterly cold February killed much of the winter wheat, which had to be undersown with another crop in the spring, yet another task at one of the busiest times of the year. Nevertheless, by April 1940, the ploughing-up campaign had reached its target and the United Kingdom had over two million acres of new arable land. Only eight counties failed to reach their target, usually because the land had been unworkable, as in Essex, under quota by some 13,000 acres, where the heavy clays were in turn hopelessly sticky and rock hard, so that it was often impossible to use a plough at all.

In the spring of 1940, the 'battle for wheat' came to seem even more vital as the phoney war was ended by the German offensive in Europe. In the struggle to make Britain self-sufficient in food, farmers were handicapped by lack of capital and credit and by scarcity of labour and equipment. Within a month of the outbreak of war, farmers were already claiming that the newly stabilised prices did not match the almost daily rises in their production costs. In September 1939, W.H. Pitts, the Vice-President of the West Sussex Branch of the N.F.U. (National Farmers' Union) had protested in *The Farmers Weekly* that the government looked upon the agricultural industry as 'a sort of philanthropic society'. It was not until the summer of 1940 that a more coherent price policy gradually emerged to give farmers a profit which could be ploughed back into the land to raise output still further. A new price schedule issued in August 1940 failed to win the approval of the N.F.U., and, by November, the government felt it had to guarantee both prices and market for the main farm products until a year after the end of the war. During 1940, the War Ags were authorised to make loans to impecunious farmers with no other sources of credit on condition that the money was repaid after the next harvest. Under this scheme a farmer could borrow up to £50 (later £100) at five per cent interest. The loans were not widely taken up, perhaps because the price awards were providing adequate working capital for expansion.

Lack of labour was often a worse worry. Two decades of rural depopulation, followed by an intensive army recruitment campaign in the spring of 1939 and then by conscription, had left a deficit of about 50,000 farm workers. Once they were over 21, farm workers were considered as being in a reserved occupation and thus exempt from conscription, but the 20,000 who had joined the Territorial Army were nevertheless called up. A.G. Street wrote in *The Farmers Weekly* on 15th September 1939 that 'a week or so ago I was running my farm with a regular staff of two lads of sixteen, three old-age pensioners, and one man aged thirty-nine. The last-mentioned was my foreman-driver, head dairyman and the only employee capable of running machinery – a veritable Admirable Crichton. Alas! he was a reservist with some three months' time unexpired. Consequently, at a moment's notice on September 1, he descended from the tractor

Government advertisements in *The Farmer & Stock-breeder*. On 26th March 1940, farmers are again urged to plough: 'The more we can grow, the more we can spend on munitions. Grow your own feeding stuffs.' On 30th April, the message is to make silage and 'make the most of your grass.'

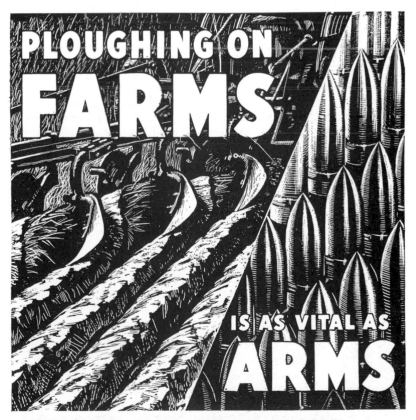

seat, and joined his unit in the North. Well, that was that, and from that moment I had been taking his place with more or less success.'

Among those drafted in to replace the missing agricultural workers were members of the Women's Land Army, reborn on 1st July 1939 after its service during World War I. By the outbreak of war, over 17,000 women had been enrolled and hundreds of applications were being received each day. The idea of inexperienced town girls helping out on the land predictably met with early hostility from both farmers and labourers, especially when it was discovered that they were to be paid a regulation wage of 28 shillings per week. In July 1939, an editorial in *The Land Worker*, the official publication of the National Union of Agricultural Workers, grumbled that 'the Hon. Mrs This, Lady That and the Countess of Something Else are all on the war path again. The Women's Land Army is here, and they have all got their old jobs back – of bossing people, and of seeing that the farmers find a way out of their labour shortage without having to pay better wages.'

A.G. Street, preoccupied with the hazards of tractor-driving, had definite views on the subject:

The modern outfit [the tractor-plough] is a one-man job, requiring an expert in both branches, an engineer and a ploughman. He works alone, perhaps miles from the nearest human being. Therefore, he must not only be an expert, but also physically capable of the strength necessary to cope with the various jobs to which even the most modern tractor and plough are heirs.

A volunteer land worker, carrying her gas mask, helps with the harvest in Hertfordshire in September 1939.

According to the original caption, dated 14th November 1939, 'Many society girls are playing their part in this war and among them is Miss Joan Street, who has joined Britain's biggest battalion of the Women's Land Army, namely Hampshire. Miss Street is the daughter of Lady Tottenham, wife of Vice-Admiral Sir Francis Loftus Tottenham.'

16

Soldiers stand in for land-workers who have been called up, Cheshire, September 1939.

That there are some land girls physically capable of dealing with these I am well aware, but I insist that the average girl is not fitted for such work. While the plough is working correctly, any girl can drive the tractor merrily up and down the field, but when things go wrong a considerable amount of sheer physical strength is often required, for, as I say, there is no other help for miles.

To my mind, even the starting of the average tractor is not a job which the average girl should be asked to do. For that matter on a cold morning it is not one which the average man – taking myself as average – should be asked to do either.

A more vehement opinion was voiced by W.R. Nicholson:

Women can look after chickens, but they cannot ditch. They can feed the pigs, but they cannot look after the boar. They can milk the cows, and, if they have enough experience, which is not very often, they can attend to their calving, but they cannot look after the bull. They can drive a tractor with a hay-sweep or hay-mower, but they cannot pitch hay. They can drive a reaper and binder, but they cannot drive a big track-laying tractor. They cannot lay drains, they cannot cart or spread chalk, or spread dung or load it. They cannot pull swedes or mangolds or load them. In fact, they cannot do any heavy work on the farm, and there is not a great deal of light work; the idea of substituting women for men on the farm is absurd.

In the event, the weather in October and November was so bad that it not merely reduced the call for Land Girls but caused some

17

male workers to be laid off for the winter months. Out of 25,000 women enrolled in the service by November, only 1,000 had been placed on farms. Miss Calmedy-Hamlyn of Bridestowe in Devon, a well-known farmer and breeder of pedigree stock, retired from the County's W.L.A. Organising Committee stating:

I feel that I have been deluded into recruiting girls and getting them to throw up their work, believing that they would get fed, clothed, trained and placed in suitable work on farms. Now they have found that there are no jobs, no uniforms, and no places for them. They are being turned adrift, while we who are the organisers of the Land Army are having our right of free speech stifled by being prevented from criticising these things we know are taking place.

Employment prospects improved somewhat in the spring, as the amount of work to be done on the farm increased and farmers discovered that Land Girls were a good deal tougher and more capable than they had imagined. By the end of May 1940, the number at work had risen to 6,000, although demand was still largely concentrated in the southern counties.

Even though the supply of Land Girls greatly exceeded the demand, other sources of extra labour were also tried. One, much canvassed in the press, was what could amount to a Youth Land Army, with schoolboys spending two or three weeks of their summer holidays helping farmers with the harvest. Among the several bodies with this aim in the spring of 1940 was the West of England Volunteer Harvesters' Association, which was made up of about 130 public and secondary schools in seven counties and undertook to assign willing boys to the farms where they were most needed. In mid April, the Minister of Agriculture announced a national plan to establish 'holiday farming camps' all over the country for boys who were still at school, while those who had left, particularly the eighteen-year-olds faced with a two-year gap before they were called up, were to be offered training in agriculture.

Just in case this plan might seem to have worrying precedents in Germany, the Minister of Agriculture explained:

There is no question of 'conscripting' youths on Nazi lines, nor will the plan involve any regimentation of youth labour. The idea is to invite these young men to offer themselves for farm work at their local Employment Exchange where they will be placed with farmers who are willing to accept their services.

A Land Girl practises decarbonising a tractor on a Lancashire County Council farm. Clearly aware of the glut of Land Girls, the caption writer in October 1939 comments: 'Women's Land Army, like the forces and other branches of National Service, cannot absorb instantaneously all the recruits it will eventually need. It will be some time before the farmers become really short of men, and in the meantime the Women's Land Army are undergoing their training in batches month by month.'

In a cabbage field at Old Bexley, Kent in June 1940, the celebrated lepidopterist L. Hugh Newman examines a haul of cabbage white butterflies with one of the bands of children he has organised to catch these pests.

Ploughing with a static steam engine as the source of power, April 1940.

A cartoon in *The Land Worker* for August 1939 expresses the NUAW's view of the relationship between agricultural wages and Government support of farming.

However, farmers were as chary of employing schoolboys as they had been of taking on women, and several of the voluntary schemes fell through in the course of the summer. While many farmers were pleased by the willingness of their young helpers, there were inevitably complaints. One farmer telephoned the Labour Committee to protest that a master in charge of a camp had refused to allow his boys to spread sludge, while another grumbled that the four lads who had been working on his farm had been 'larking about'. Even so, the experiment worked well enough to be repeated in later years.

The real problem, though, was the continued loss of skilled agricultural workers, now tempted away from the land into higher paid war work – they could easily double or treble their wages building military camps, aerodromes and factories. On 17th November 1939, *The Farmers Weekly* carried the following story:

An acquaintance of mine who farms in an area that has recently assumed a very pronounced military character lost his cowman a few months ago. The man had worked on the farm for many years at the normal rate of 35s. a week.

Last week the erstwhile cowman made a call on his former employer, 'Just to see how things were going,' as he put it. He drove up in a very smart car.

The farmer was a wee bit taken aback when he saw the car. Says he: 'Whose car?'

'Mine,' said the ex-cowman proudly.

'Where d'you get it?'

'Bought it – and it's paid for.'

'Yes, but where where d'you get the money?'

'Earned it, of course.'

'But where?'

'Oh, I'm working on the army camp over at – –. I never knock out less than £6 a week now.'

This may have been above the national average of about £4 a week, but both compared handsomely with the farm wage which in March 1940 averaged about 38s. a week, although farm labourers did enjoy some perks – a tied cottage, free milk and perhaps an allotment. At its annual conference two months later, the National Union of Agricultural Workers demanded 60s. a week, a move strongly resisted

19

by the National Farmers' Union, which offered 40s. and in the end agreed to a compromise figure of 48s. This was introduced as a statutory minimum wage from July 1940. As pay alone was still not going to be enough to keep farm workers on the land, the government also took action to stop employers in other trades from taking on men from agriculture, and again reduced the age at which farming became a reserved occupation, this time from 21 to 18. This protection from being called up succeeded in bringing men back to the farms and helped avert the widely feared labour shortage.

With the Labour Exchanges more than able to supply the necessary workers and with greater use of machinery, the hot, dry summer of 1940 ended in a bumper harvest, some ten per cent higher than the average in the late 1930s.

For the next year a target was set of one and three quarter million acres to be newly ploughed up. Apart from wheat and potatoes, both of which had done well in 1940, special encouragement was to be given to growing vegetables, particularly tomatoes and carrots. In addition, the Government wished to increase the acreage of flax to replace supplies from the Baltic and the Low Countries. Flax provided a tough fibre that could be made up into linen, tent canvas, the fabric used on aircraft wings, webbing for parachute harnesses and fire hoses, ropes and thread. Linseed oil from flax was an important addition to home-grown animal feeding stuffs.

November 1940: women collecting potatoes that have already been turned out of the ground. On the suggestion of the Ministry of Agriculture, the potatoes have been left longer than usual to grow large.

Just after eight o'clock in the evening in July 1940, haymaking at Law Wood, Windermere, in the Lake District.

Surprisingly, the number of livestock kept on British farms hardly changed during the first year of the war. By the autumn of 1940, though, farmers were worried that the worsening import situation would leave them without enough feed to overwinter all their animals. So many fat cattle, sheep and pigs were sent for slaughter that the markets were swamped and the meat ration had to be raised until after Christmas. The result was a new government livestock policy aimed at preventing another glut and, as far as possible, maintaining reserves of meat on the hoof. A feed rationing scheme was introduced in February 1941 giving priority to high-yielding dairy cows.

The multitude of government directives were carried out at a local level largely by the War Ags. These started as committees of eight to ten farmers and other agriculturalists who then appointed sub-committees to deal with labour, machinery, feeding stuffs and so on. Despite Lord Beaverbrook's misgivings ('You cannot milk a cow by committees. A cow has only got four teats'), the War Ags proved to be effective and were strengthened in May 1940 by bringing in salaried staff from the County Farm Institutes to act as scientific and technical advisers, and later by the appointment of liaison officers to keep the Minister informed of what was happening in the regions.

One of the early tasks of the War Ags was to inspect all the farms in the country in the summer of 1940 and produce a New Domesday Survey to record what each was producing and what was needed to extract the maximum yield. Farmers were divided into A, B and C categories corresponding to those who farmed well, moderately well and badly. The aim was to advise and encourage them, rather than anything more drastic. So, when Louis Goddard of Thornland Farm at Hockworth in Devon was visited by representatives of his Committee, he was complimented on his efforts with his 57-acre holding and asked if there were any problems. Was he short of labour? 'I've got a man comes over three days a week,' replied Goddard. 'One time we had a girl in the house, and she used to help. But she died.' The return made by the War Ag stated that the farmer required a single man or temporarily a land girl, if she could milk.

A demonstration of straw pulp making held by the Yorkshire War Ag in November 1941.

Inevitably, many farmers disliked being told what to do with their land, particularly by neighbouring farmers charged with walking the farm and passing judgement on the standard of husbandry. But the direction of the War Ags was thought necessary to overcome any reluctance to take productive land out of use and wait for as much as a year or two for a cereal crop, meanwhile incurring extra costs, for example in ploughing up grassland. Although increased prices and the arable subsidy were an incentive, there were those who had to be badgered into producing crops they were not used to and C category farmers who needed more than cajoling to become acceptable B farmers.

One who benefited from the attentions of the country War Ag was John Lovick of the Breck Farm at Swannington in Norfolk who went on the wireless in the spring of 1942 to describe how his lot had improved since 1939:

We lived – my wife and I – mainly on the produce of our poultry and the milk from two cows. One dry year then would have broken me for good. I'd completely lost my confidence in farming. My wife turned to her needle, and by playing the organ in church helped all she could.

In 1939 my 60 acres only produced 46 sacks of grain and 24 tons of sugar beet. I was one of the first Norfolk farmers to be reported to the County Committee. I didn't like that, I admit, so I wrote a letter and went off on my bike in the snow to see our Executive Officer, Mr Rayns; he came back and went round the farm with me, and somehow I felt that he saw the difficulties. I know now that I was in danger of losing my farm. He suggested that I should consider changing my methods, and work according to his directions, and that I should accept financial assistance from the Committee. I didn't

Sowing seed by hand, May 1941.

like the idea. It was something new to me. I was given a second-hand tractor and a tractor plough – a debt I've since fully repaid – and in the winter and spring of 1940 I broke the stubbles, ploughed and drilled 60 acres of land alone. In my own workshop I turned my horse drill into a tractor drill, fitted a roller to my plough and did these two jobs together on my light land. I used some heavy doses of fertilisers, and my drillings were a month earlier. The County Committee's combine harvesters which came to cut my oats were the first that had been seen in the village.

By 1941, John Lovick's farm was producing five times as much as it had in 1939, he had taken on 20 acres of adjoining land and had a Land Girl and occasionally a man or woman from the village helping him. He was reclassified as a B farmer in 1942.

Taking advantage of the financial incentives to improve land also made sense in the long term. Captain Frank Thompson Schwab, the senior partner of a firm of stockbrokers, who farmed 700 acres in Cumberland, ploughed up and reseeded 150 acres of rough grazing land, removing hundreds of tons of rock in the process. In 1942 he reported: 'Not only is this land producing *ten* times more than it did before, but its value has increased from pre-war values of £2 per acre of land to £15, and the cost of reclamation, after allowing for Government subsidies, has not been more than £5.

Persistent inefficiency or failure to comply with the Committee's directives could at the very least result in a fine. In March 1940, a

Below: planting leek seeds with a hand-drill at Evesham, Worcestershire, February 1941. Right: drilling mangold seed, Grazeley, near Reading, May 1941.

Northamptonshire farmer, Harry Kimbell, had to pay £20 with five guineas costs for failing to plough up 62½ acres when instructed to do so by the County War Ag. Kimbell claimed in his defence that ploughing and sowing his heavy, wet land was useless during the winter months as 'no-one but a mad man would expect a crop from the land, it wants a summer fallow.' Despite his long tenure of the farm, his explanation was not accepted by the Committee. Inevitably, there were cases where Committees abused their authority, which extended to the right to take possession of the farms and cultivate them directly for the duration of the war and for five years thereafter. Thus, in May 1941, a farmer at Malmesbury in Wiltshire was given only six days to leave his land on grounds of under-production, after holding it for 35 years without complaint. Two months later, Mr Mason, who farmed at Birdsall in Yorkshire, was forcibly ejected from his holding for not carrying out the East Riding War Ag's instruction on manuring. A question in the House of Commons asking whether Mr Mason had been given an opportunity to continue in some capacity on his farm or to remain in his farmhouse received the reply: 'He has certainly been evicted from the house because it is required for the new tenant. I do not know what he is going to do in the future.'

Just how harsh the procedure could be is shown in this eviction order delivered to Alfred Howell, a dairy farmer of Hawthorne Farm, Chartridge, Great Missenden, Buckinghamshire, in November 1942:

(1) If by Friday, November 20, 1942, you have not vacated the holding, the Executive Committee, with the assistance of the police, will remove the furniture from the dwelling house and place it either in one room of the house or in one of the farm buildings, where it will remain at your risk.
(2) The Committee will remove the farm implements into one of the farm buildings, where they will remain again at your own risk.
(3) The Executive Committee will, having received the consent of the Minister of Agriculture, requisition any livestock which may be found on the holding; such livestock will be requisitioned and conveyed to Aylesbury and sold in the market on Saturday, November 21. The proceeds of such sale will be held against your claim for compensation.

For some, the disgrace and worry about the future was too much, and there were several suicides among dispossessed farmers. Only a few opted to resist and go down fighting. In April 1940, a Hampshire farmer refused to obey a ploughing directive from the County Committee, considering it to be ill-judged, and similarly ignored an eviction order issued in July. The police were sent in, only to find the farmhouse secured against them and the farmer armed with a shotgun. After an exchange of shots and the unsuccessful use of tear gas, the police, backed up by troops, forced an entry. Continuing to resist arrest, the farmer was shot dead.

Small wonder, then, that the dictatorial attitude of the War Ags often inspired terror. One or two brave souls did manage to make an effective protest. In an extraordinary incident in 1941, a Wiltshire estate owner, Mark Dingley, was said to have fired a live shell from a trench mortar which landed in the middle of a field where members of the local War Ag were working. The Committee, having failed to reach an agreement with him over 20 acres of land of Manor Farm, Berwick St John, served possession notices on him. Dingley had written to the Committee informing them that he did not want his land 'mucked about by office boys and civil servants who know nothing.' When the men from the War Ag arrived on his land on 6th

Threshing oats by hand with a flail, Westmorland, February 1941.

December, Dingley told them that they were trespassers and warned them off. A fortnight later, he told them again, underlining his point by firing a mortar followed by a Mills hand grenade, which burst 40 yards away. Even so, he got away with fines of £10 on each of two summonses at Tisbury Police Court, with £3.17s costs.

The sad truth was that few small farmers possessed the means or influence to contest an official decision. In all, about 15,000 farmers were forcibly dispossesed – not many, perhaps, out of some 350,000 agricultural holdings, but for them and their families the result was virtual ruination. There was no right of appeal, and resentment was

Government advertising in 1941 again stressed the urgency of ploughing. This advertisement, which appeared in *The Field* in August exhorted farmers: 'Start NOW, or demands on available machinery will be too great next Spring. Early ploughing means early sowing and early sowing means better crops.'

Time is food –
PLOUGH *NOW!*

– between the stooks if possible

made worse by the Minister of Agriculture's blank refusal to review the procedures. A Dispossessed Farmers Supporters' Association was set up to seek redress and held its inaugural meeting in December 1944. It eventually attracted some 5,000 members and lasted for about six years, although it achieved comparatively little. Bitter memories endured long after. Francis Mountford, whose father was evicted in 1942 and became a labourer in an aluminium factory, recollected in 1985:

My family is still in touch with the families of two or three others, although most of the original dispossessed are now dead. We, the older children, will never forget those worrying days when we dreaded that day of leaving coming, and wondered what would become of us when it arrived. This, for me, was the war-time memory above all others. I am still indignant at the injustice of our dispossession and at the inhumanity of authorities that provided no financial help for the farmers to do the work which they ordered to be carried out; and no compensation, house, job nor anything at all to those whom they turned out. Twenty years after we left the farm the work which my father had been ordered to do, which was the reason for his dispossession, had still not been carried out!

Such casualties were perhaps inevitable in the battle for production, but in the main the War Ags could be proud of their record in requisitioning over 300,000 unproductive areas and bringing them swiftly into cultivation. One of the largest tasks was the reclamation of derelict land, such as the 5,000 acres in East Suffolk reported as supporting only 'tall scrub and hedges that are superabundant as to their height and width.'

The Essex War Ag undertook the draining and ditching of some 20,000 acres in the county, much of it stiff and unyielding London clay, in an attempt to restore the capital's natural granary. But the efforts went far beyond field drainage, involving collaboration with the river catchment boards to undertake ambitious draining schemes in the wetlands such as the Norfolk Fens at Feltwell, Hockwell and Lakenheath, of which some 6,000 acres were brought into cultivation. In the Trent Valley of Nottinghamshire a total of £16,000 was spent on new pumping stations to drain 4,000 acres of marshland and a further £100,000 in constructing new roads and a system of modern water courses parallel with the 17th-century ditches of the Dutchman Vermuiden. These efforts, however, were dwarfed by that of the Somerset Catchment Board which laid out nearly £400,000 on improving the drainage of 100,000 acres of flat land

Land girls working self-binders on the Sussex Downs in August 1941. The 400-acre wheat field, believed to be Britain's largest, was produced from derelict land that had not been ploughed for twenty years.

within its area. The work included cutting a canal nearly five miles long and deepening and widening the King's Sedgemoor Drain, which had originally been cut in 1795.

In upland areas, too, the War Ags were extending cultivation to unproductive land, some of which had not seen the plough since Napoleonic times. Particularly energetic in this respect was the East Sussex Committee, which set its sights on ploughing several thousand acres of the South Downs, grassland in such a state of neglect that it was considered worthless other than for 'harbouring rabbits, vermin and wild life.' This work, which irrevocably changed the face of the South Downs, was tackled as a military operation and quickly produced creditable yields. Equally well publicised but not as successful was the Montgomeryshire War Ag's attempt to grow potatoes on Dolfer Hill, 1,500 ft up in the Welsh mountains. In 1941 the bracken and gorse that covered the slopes were attacked with an array of enormous machines including a Massey Harris 'Prairie Buster' (one of only three in the country) as well as several Ransomes 'Jumbotrac', three-furrow deep digger ploughs drawn by the newly developed Allis Chalmers supercharged diesel tractors, giants of their kind, weighing nearly six tons. Nevertheless, the scheme was a failure, as the land was severely deficient in lime and phosphate. The poor yields persuaded the Committee to modify its programme and re-seed the land to produce good quality grazing. But towards the end of the war, the government was growing increasingly cost-conscious, wanting to exert closer control over the work of the War Ags, and the Montgomery Committee was sacked in the autumn of 1944.

Apart from its efforts in reclaiming land for cereal and vegetable cultivation, the Government also wanted to improve the quality of the remaining grassland as a reservoir of soil fertility. Research had shown that the keynote of good husbandry was the establishment of temporary grass leys rich in leguminous plants which avoided over-cropping and sustained the natural fertility of the land. Ley farming was strongly supported by the various War Ags from 1942, as it seemed to be the best solution for the dual problem of impoverished soil and inadequate fertiliser supplies.

A 'fireside chat' organised by the Technical Development sub-committee of the Montgomeryshire War Ag in April 1943. At the extreme left is J.L. John, the County Agricultural Adviser.

Left: dumping lime on land at Underbarrow, Westmorland, in February 1942.

Right: a new type of orchard spraying machine using a tar-oil emulsion to destròy three kinds of fruit tree pest being demonstrated in Cambridgeshire, December 1942.

The inevitable consequence of falling livestock numbers was less dung, and the reduction in the amount of the imported oil cake in the diet of the farm animals meant that the dung that was produced was of inferior quality. This could be compensated for by increased use of artificial fertilisers, but by the second half of 1940 there was a shortage of imported phosphates and potash. Both were subsequently rationed, and only home-produced nitrogenous fertilisers were in sufficient supply until 1943.

Even when there was enough artificial fertiliser to go round, less was used than the Government wished. Some enterprising souls declared boldly that they could farm without muck, but many doubted that artificial fertilisers could keep the land in good heart, believing, as Colonel Pollit put it in April 1943, that 'the only successful foundation of farming is farmyard manure.' Others backed the use of sewage, sludge and other domestic wastes as an alternative to chemicals, but in only a few places, such as Maidenhead in Berkshire and Leatherhead in Surrey, was a practicable scheme worked out. In the end, though, the scientific revolution, which extended beyond fertilisers to new means of pest, disease and weed control, was irresistible, though an editorial in *The Farmers Weekly* as late as 6th April 1945 was expressing reservations which might well be echoed today:

Digging out sludge from a sewage settling tank before layering it with straw in an experimental scheme in Hampshire, December 1943.

Right: traditional pest control – watched by a sheepdog, boys and terriers search for rats in the bottom of a corn stack during threshing, Westmorland, January 1941.

Ploughing the Eppynt Hills of Brecon, 1,400 feet above sea-level at Ty-Capel, land said not to have been broken since the days of the wooden plough drawn by oxen. June 1940.

Caterpillar crawler tractor, photographed in April 1944.

This age of marvels! M. and B., penicillin, D.D.T., gammexane and methoxone, all super-super-bug killers and all devised and produced (like the flying bomb and the rocket bomb), to the glory of god-like man.

The latest in this seeming catalogue of an apothecary's nightmare is methoxone which will apparently clear weeds out of corn with unparalleled completeness.

Maybe I'm old-fashioned, but I find all this progress somehow frightening. I don't know how or why but I feel you cannot upset a logical balance of nature without her getting her own back on you.

May she not retaliate, for instance, by increasing the weeds in those fields, roots and green vegetables, where, we are told, we must not use the new weed killer.

Farmers were generally more receptive to the new machinery, but there was not enough of that to go around. The principal source of supply, once the Lend-Lease agreements with the United States came into operation in the spring of 1941, was American. Imports included powerful crawler tractors (needed on the stiff clays), disc harrows to break up grassland, binders and combines to gather the much improved corn harvest, and the newly-developed potato harvesters. *Country Life* commented:

What impresses the layman is the number of new tractors at work on land. The bright ochre Fordson, the yellow 'Caterpillar' and the scarlet International and Massey Harris stand out. Altogether, we have just over 80,000 tractors on farms in this country, and at least 30,000 of them are new ones with a show of paint. It is only because

30

International combine harvester near Teffont Magna, Wiltshire, September 1939.

R. Douglas, a market gardener from Worthing, Sussex, still using in August 1943 what was said to be the oldest working motor-driven plough in Britain, a World War I model.

we have been able to get these extra tractors that the gigantic job of the second year's ploughing campaign on top of the first has been managed so well.

Even so, the shortage of tractors led to an enormous boom in secondhand machinery, which sold for as much as or even more than new. One War Ag had twenty new tractors to allocate at the controlled price of £215 apiece, and there were 106 applications. Three days after the tractors had been allocated, a secondhand machine of similar make and less than mint condition became available in the same county and fetched £355 at auction. Even World War I models were pressed back into service, and the shortage of implements to go with the new tractors led to all manner of ingenious hitches and shackles to attach the old horse-drawn equipment.

Machinery for market gardening: a Rototiller being used to prepare the ground for lettuce planting near Newport, Monmouthshire, in April 1940.

Horse-power also came back into fashion, but horses, too, were in short supply. By the 'thirties, town and army transport were mechanised, and the breeding of draught horses had ceased to be a profitable enterprise – even in agriculture fewer horses were needed in the years before the war, with so much acreage given over to grass. The ploughing-up campaigns, however, sent horse prices rocketing. After a sale at which a couple of three-year-olds made £200 and £140 respectively and a six-year-old £132, a correspondent from *The Farmers Weekly* heard a Scottish farm manager comment:

Two or three years syne naebody wanted horses. They were out o' date. Stinking tractors was what everyone wanted, maybe because there was a canny bit seat on them; they were easy to drive, no' like a pair of banging horses; they didna eat any guid oats or hay when they weren't working, nor did they need any muckin' oot at weekends.

Now they are all tumblin' over one another to get horse flesh and they've got out of the way o' kennin' a guid one when they see one . . .

You watch what happens. They'll be gie'n a hundred pound for a beast wi' three legs, a broken wind, and a stifle oot. And they'll find when they get the beast hame that they canna get a new stifle as a new spare part at the garage or the smithy, or send for a mechanic tae to put new bellows in an auld nag. It's just how they bin brought up, they ken nae better.

Left: a plough maker takes advantage of the tractor shortage to advertise his products. Right: the Ministry of Supply appeals in *The Farmers Weekly* of 19th June 1942 for scrap rubber: 'The enemy now holds 90% of the world's natural rubber resources. That is why every scrap of rubber lying useless and discarded all over the country is wanted for war purposes – at once!' A checklist provided of items made of rubber includes grain drill tubes, nest boxes, potato digger prongs, sheep boots and tree ties.

Horse-power at work, ploughing on the South Oxfordshire Hills in November 1942.

When he had heard the prices that horses were fetching, he added, 'Did I no' tell ye? The whole wairrld's gone daft!' Most farmers, though, preferred tractors for their quicker operation and their greater working capacity. Anyway, 'ready-made' horses like the three-year-olds at the auction were more often a liability than an asset, and finding men with the experience to school them was no longer easy.

Machinery supplies slowed down again after the entry of the United States into the war in December 1941, when much of the U.S. tractor industry was turned over to the production of tanks and armaments. Much of the machinery promised for the 1942 harvest came too late, while the 1943 schedule was considerably reduced, as the build-up for a major European offensive had reduced American farm machinery production to a fifth of its 1941 level, while the output of wheeled tractors was only a tenth of what it had been two years earlier. Some of the deficit was made up by British manufacturers, but their efforts were hampered by shortage of raw materials. The shortages were made worse by Japanese advances: the invasion of Java and Malaya, the world's main sources of rubber, led to a dearth of pneumatic tyres, while the fall of the Philippines cut off imports of hemp, which was used in binder twine. From the end of 1942, twine was for use only in binding machines and not for other farm purposes. From August 1943, all new farm machinery was rationed. Manufacturers had to comply with official instructions over the models and quantities they produced, and dealers supplied the listed machines only to farmers whose applications had been approved by the War Ags. To fill the gaps, farmers could usually hire equipment from their War Ag or perhaps from a locally organised machinery pool like the 'Help Your Neighbour' scheme set up in ten parishes in the East Riding of Yorkshire in September 1942. At seasonal peaks, tractor-power would be used 24 hours a day, with the drivers working in shifts, which was not without its hazards because of the wartime restrictions on the vehicle headlights. The Ministry of Agriculture considered that 'straightforward work . . . can be carried on successfully using a masked motor car headlamp shining to the front and another similarly directed to the rear of the plough.'

33

Such efforts dramatically increased the acreage under cultivation each year up to 1943. The main disappointment was failure to reach the quota for flax. Many farmers were unwilling to grow it unless directed to do so. It required a fertile soil, was sensitive to drought and needed experience to produce decent yields. Harvesting it by hand was a tedious and back-breaking business, and mechanical flax harvesters were only just being introduced.

A particular concern of 1942 was the shortage of milk. In a drive to raise output, the farmers were encouraged to arrange more calvings for the autumn and to grow more winter feed, particularly beans. As an incentive, a series of 'Victory Churns' contests was arranged and trophies awarded for the greatest increase in milk sales; perhaps more significantly, the farm price of milk was increased. The six per cent increase in milk production for the year 1942-43 was not enough to satisfy the growing demand for milk, but it at least reversed the downward trend.

The most severe food crisis came in the winter of 1942-43, because of the shipping situation. Sinkings of merchantmen were high, and it was only towards the end of 1942 that replacements began to outstrip losses. Even then, the new ships were needed for carrying troops rather than food. American assistance was not forthcoming in the necessary quantities, as the priority was now the success of the Torch offensive in North Africa. By January 1943, imports were down to half a million tons, the lowest of the war. Matters improved in the spring – May was a decisive month in overcoming the U-boats, and allied forces were soon to assume control of the Mediterranean. The American ship-building industry was also reaching its peak, making possible more imports of food and raw materials in American ships and others allocated to Britain under the 'bare-boat' charter.

Nevertheless, the Government was still sufficiently anxious about the food situation that it asked home agriculture to surpass all previous achievements in 1943. The target was for over 600,000 acres more wheat, and at least a ten per cent increase in potatoes and other vegetables, as much sugar beet as the previous year, and the greatest possible amount of milk. Another million acres of permanent grass were to be ploughed up, and the War Ags were told that this was the crisis year and that farmers should strain every sinew to ensure a record harvest, without regard to the effects on the soil fertility or output in subsequent years. The production of meat would inevitably fall, but this could not be helped. As Lord Woolton, the Minister of Food, stated in an interview in *The Farmers Weekly* of 11th December 1942, 'The need is so great that farmers must be prepared to deliver the grain to the nation at the expense of their pockets, their land and even their animals.'

The new targets were thought possible if increased resources were made available. In 1940, farmers' fear about a shortage of manpower had proved unfounded, but the needs of the armed forces had made this a reality by 1941. In March, the age at which farming became a reserved occupation was raised to 25, allowing some 10,000 men to be taken from agriculture into the services during the following year and the siphoning-off of younger men continued steadily thereafter, although not all who were eligible for conscription went, as farmers were allowed to apply to the War Ags to keep key personnel – each case was decided on its merits. Even so, there were not enough experienced men to go around and the auxiliary workers, particularly the Women's Land Army, made a crucial contribution.

By 1941, much of the initial hostility to the Land Girls had been overcome, and there was little difficulty in finding places for its 20,000 recruits, a number which rapidly doubled after the Government's announcement in January 1942 that women would be liable

"I know Mr. Hudson has worked miracles, but I can't produce anything until February and then only twins at most."

Cartoons in *The Farmer & Stock-breeder* in December 1941 comment on the food production drive led by Lord Woolton, the Minister of Food, and Robert Hudson, the Minister of Agriculture.

HARVESTING

MILITARY MACHINE

farm labour

LOW

In a September 1941 cartoon, David Low encapsulates the problem of labour on the land in his image of a combine harvester driven by Blimps swallowing up farm workers.

for compulsory war work under the direction of the Ministry of Labour. The task of turning shop assistants, hairdressers, typists and waitresses into useful farm hands was undertaken by the County Farm Institutes, the War Ags and the farmers themselves. Aspiring Land Girls were typically grouped in batches of thirty to forty and given a four or five week initial course in all types of farming at somewhere like the Northamptonshire Farm Institute at Moulton. Some recruits, however, were subjected to a harsher regime, away from the school at specially selected farms. One such place was described by *Illustrated* magazine on 13th December 1941:

At a place fourteen miles from civilization, a thousand feet above sea level, surrounded by moorland country, is Harehills Farm. Here are trained girls who are going to become the toughest land girls, the girls who are going out to farms to do men's work – as well as men could do it.

The girls are hand-picked by Mrs Edythe Marsden, western representative of the Women's Land Army. She chooses them for their mental as well as their physical ability. Their first test is the lonely walk up to the farm – a test which many a city girl might fear.

But most of the girls come from the cities and industrial towns. They arrive unsuitably shod, unsuitably clad; with four-inch heels and eye-veils.

Make-up masks their faces. They are finicky about their food on that first evening.

But next morning the scene changes. Up at 5.30, the girls wash in cold water. Then out to milk the cows. Breakfast at eight. Off to the fields at 8.30 until 4 o'clock with half an hour's break for midday dinner. After a twenty-minute tea they go milking again. Then the shippons [cattle-sheds] and the dairy have to be cleaned.

While they are training the girls get 10 shillings a week allowance and full farming kit. Later, when they are fully trained, they earn 39s 8d a week without board.

Some girls received no training – they simply learned on the job and through their mistakes. Volunteers had to be mobile and to go without protest wherever they were sent. This might be to a hostel, from where they were sent from farm to farm as required, or it might be to fill a particular vacancy for a Land Girl. The greatest demand

At a training school for W.L.A. forewomen run by the Hertfordshire War Ag in the clubhouse of the Herts Golf Club, Miss E. Chiavassa, who made baby cots before the war, teaches Land Girls the art of digging ditches in June 1943.

was for milkers, but the Land Girl might be expected to help with the field work – ploughing, weeding and hoeing, dung spreading – and then with the harvests of hay, corn, potatoes and root vegetables. During the winter, there were hedges to trim and ditches to clear out. Most of the work was hard and often undertaken under atrocious conditions. Just as in the army, there were specialist trades to which personnel could be drafted. Girls might specialise in, for instance, fruit culture, market gardening, or pest control which could mean rat catching. Mrs Sylvia Knight remembers how she decided to become 'a lady killer of vermin' in Lincolnshire:

It was a choice of dairy work or rat catching. I thought the latter would be more interesting and it was not for seven days a week. My mother was horrified when I told her.

I was sent to Addlethorpe, near Skegness, for instruction. We had classroom lectures given by Professor Ashton, who was attached to Oxford University, and who made the subject of rodents quite fascinating. After the lectures we were taken to put our newly acquired knowledge into practice. We went to a nearby village and on to premises where circus animals and sideshow animals (such as five-legged calves) were being housed for the duration. Professor Ashton gave us each a number, mine was 10, and when he shouted that I

Mrs Addison, a 63-year-old grandmother in the W.L.A., tightens nuts on her tractor after draining the sump. In November 1939, she has just completed a four-week tractor training course in Essex.

36

Land Girls bagging their morning catch of rats on a Devon farm. 70 out of the 72 Land Girls working on pest destruction in Devon came from Yorkshire.

Training Land Girls in Buckinghamshire to maintain a Fordson tractor and in Suffolk to milk.

was to stand in a shallow, smelly dyke and then to put my arm down a nearby rat hole. It made my flesh creep, but with true Yorkshire grit I obeyed. When I plunged my arm in quickly and yelled out which way the hole ran, withdrawing with even greater speed. The girls on top of the bank started pumping cymag gas into another hole (the pump resembled a stirrup pump). Seconds later a huge rat ran out of my hole, incidentally the first I had ever seen. The shock was great and I landed on my back in the smelly drain. The reason why the site was overrun with rats was because there were two lion carcases lying a few yards away . . .

After this not too great a start, I was fortunate enough to pass the tests and was sent to North Somercotes (Lincolnshire) to join two other girls. We killed rabbits, crows, moles and mice besides rats.

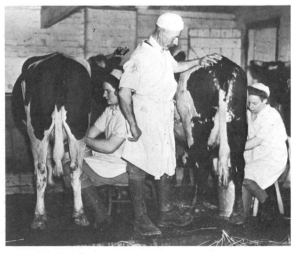

Hostel for Land Girls, April 1943 –
the drapes around the windows are
painted.

We used a number of different poisons – arsenic, red squill, barium carbonate, zinc phosphide, plus cymag gas. They were certainly more effective than their modern equivalents.

It was an unusual occupation, but I enjoyed the experience, and I ended up by having a lot of admiration for rats – for their tenacity and will to live.

Such squads could achieve formidable results. Four North Wales Land Girls, travelling around by bicycle, were reported to have destroyed no fewer than 35,545 rabbits, 7,689 rats, 1,668 foxes and 1,901 moles between February 1941 and April 1942. This achievement was considered to have been a record.

For seasonal work peaks, Land Girls were formed into mobile gangs. In 1942 the Wiltshire War Ag employed 26 of these mobile gangs for threshing, while in Kent all the threshing gangs were female. A.G. Street went to watch the gangs at work in Wiltshire:

Recently, on a drizzly, cold afternoon, I visited several gangs. I saw typists minding the chaff, mannequins on the straw rick, bank clerks

Opposite page, clockwise from top left. Playing darts during the festive season at the W.L.A. Forestry Camp at Culford in Suffolk. Selecting potato tubers for planting at the W.L.A. Forewomen's Training Camp in Hertfordshire, April 1943. Carting dung at Cannington, near Bridgwater in Somerset. Sawing logs. Planting potatoes on reclaimed land at Holkham Marshes, Norfolk, March 1944. Turning hay before stacking at Artington Manor Farm, near Guildford in Surrey, July 1942.

Land Girls hoeing onions at a farm in the Home Counties, August 1941.

Threshing near Penshurst in Kent, February 1942. At the time, over 500 Land Girls, mainly from the industrial North, were working on threshing gangs in Kent.

on the corn rick, and domestic servants cutting bonds. I saw girls with hair out of curl, girls whose hands showed the marks of their new calling, and girls with smudged faces. But I saw not a single unhappy girl, nor one that would not pass A1 physically for any service.

Of their work the farmers and regular farm workers all spoke highly. In one cow yard that I splashed through, to my query as to how the girls were doing a grizzled dairy man answered, 'Amazing, an' much better than I reckoned possible.' That was the general opinion encountered throughout my trip.

I am not suggesting that this scheme – or every gang of girls working in it – is perfect, but from personal inspection I can definitely say that it works, and also that without it the winter threshing in this wet, western county would be considerably more behind schedule than it is.

Other itinerant gangs included girls specialising in rick-thatching, heavy earth-moving work, and forestry. The Timber Corps was an offshoot of the W.L.A. and provided healthy exercise for those prepared to go out into the woods for weeks on end, selecting and marking trees for pit props and telegraph poles and replanting the cleared areas.

A farmer from the Isle of Ely in Cambridgeshire reported on the work done by his Land Girl:

1) Drives away at manure cart, etc.
2) Harrows in with one horse behind a drill
3) Loads straw when at litter-cart.
4) Holds sacks when putting up corn.
5) When chaff-cutting pushes the straw to the feeder.
6) Takes off chaff when threshing.
7) Took up quite a lot of beet, and always earned her money and a little more at £2 per acre.
8) Takes up mangolds very well.

V. Sackville-West's 1944 book on the Land Army published statistics prepared at the University College of Wales at Aberystwyth comparing work outputs of women and men. Taking the output of an adult male as 100, women scored from 42 for potato loading to 103 for pulling peas, usually reaching only the 50s or 60s for really heavy work, but managing the 70s and 80s for most other tasks and the 90s for milking, turning hay and planting and lifting potatoes.

Land girls grinding an axe before beginning tree-felling at the W.L.A. Forestry Camp at Culford in Suffolk.

Land Girl working on a drainage programme in South Warwickshire, July 1943.

Some Land Girls delighted in rivalling men at their jobs – Miss M. Wilford of Leicestershire beat all comers at an open ploughing contest at Market Bosworth in 1944. Other girls, though, discovered quite early that they had made a mistake in joining the W.L.A. One instructress at the Hampshire Farm Institute at Sparsholt bemoaned the fact that the Land Army posters showed 'a pretty girl nursing a lamb or an equally ravishing blond in a picture-hat, tossing a minute wisp of hay.' The reality was very different, and it was 'only when the girl was sent off to the farm that she realised what farm work was like – the long hours, the monotony, the loneliness, and the incredibly hard work.'

Girls who arrived ignorant and were slow or unwilling to learn soon provoked the scorn of country people – Land Girl anecdotes were almost as common as those about evacuees. There was, for instance, the story of the 'bright young thing' being shown around a Sussex farm and being told that a cow was due to calve. 'Why?' she asked. The National Union of Agricultural Workers, which was none too keen on the idea of Land Girls, commented in its magazine August 1940:

In the House of Commons . . . Mr. Lloyd George referred to 'the bad days of Eden, when Adam was turned out because he was a bad farmer.' There is no evidence of bad calculation in the Garden of Eden, the story of which contains an agricultural moral always overlooked. It was a successful holding utterly wrecked by the employment of woman's labour in the fruit-picking season.

In a manual for volunteers to the Land Army, W.E. Shewell-Cooper warned his readers of the dangers of a superior attitude:

41

Land Girls from London at Church Knowle Farm, a training centre in Dorset.

Some townspeople are apt to look upon all country folk as country bumpkins . . . Actually, country folk usually know far more than those who are born and bred in towns and cities. They may not know all the names of the film stars and the pictures in which they have appeared, but they do know the names of the birds and their habits. They are able to tell whether it is going to be wet or fine the next day. They know which herbs are useful and all about the ways of wild animals. They have a different kind of knowledge, that is all.

He also suggested restraint in the use of make-up:

Town girls on the whole use far more make-up than country girls. The Women's Land Army volunteer should therefore be prepared to 'tone down' her lips, complexion and nails considerably.

A certain amount of make-up may be used at parties and local village dances, but long nails are quite unsuited to work on a farm, especially when covered with bright crimson nail-varnish.

The volunteer will soon find that, as the other girls from the village do not use make-up, she will prefer not to use it herself, so as not to look conspicuous. She will find, too, that she will get such a healthy colour to her cheeks that rouging will not be necessary!

Even for the most willing of Land Girls, the conditions of service were exacting. The compulsory working week was 50 hours in summer and 48 hours in winter for a minimum wage of 18 shillings (later 22s 6d) after deduction of board and lodging. There was little chance of time off – a weekly half holiday, and an occasional long week-end, perhaps, if the hours were made up the previous or following week. In addition to the usual public holidays, Land Girls were entitled to a week's annual holiday with pay.

They had some protection against unsuitable billeting, as they were visited by W.L.A. district representatives, but otherwise Land Girls were thrown in at the deep end and had to depend on the good-will and commonsense of their employers. Some undoubtedly felt that they had a raw deal and were exploited by the farmers for whom they worked. Eileen Ramsey was so unlucky with her posting that she and her friend Ada Reed protested in a letter to *The Farmers Weekly* on 7th January 1943:

Land Girl breaking the ice to water cattle at Yatesbury in Wiltshire.

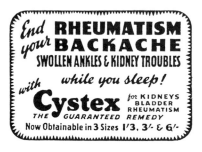
Sir, – It is generally admitted that most of the girls in the W.L.A. come from the towns. Country girls do not volunteer as they know the working conditions too well.

I am a town girl and, with a real desire to serve my country, I joined the W.L.A. My experience has been that you get very little understanding or gratitude from the farming community for doing a tough and lonely job.

After a month's training, I was sent to a well-to-do farmer in Staffordshire where, after a fortnight, I was given notice, being told that the farmer did not like Catholics and that I would be given a good reference. I later learnt the real reason for dismissal, namely that I was not the farmer's type.

My friend and I then went to a farm in Cumberland. On the night of our arrival we discussed wages and overtime and, on the farmer's

Land Army ditching team who in civilian life were a die stamper, a wine bottler, a comptometer operator and a chocolate-box maker.

Harvest time at Sandringham – Princesses Elizabeth and Margaret Rose have a word with a Land Girl working on the royal farms.

suggestion, agreed to waive overtime in exchange for a long week-end every month. We harvested until it was dark, Saturdays as well, then milked. When the harvest was gathered in, threshing done, and the potatoes up, we were told that we were not needed any longer. Incidentally, we were there three months and only got one long week-end. Our feeling is that we were exploited. The farmer's wife added insult to injury by saying, 'Any half-wit servant girl could do your job.'

And we gave up good jobs to enter the W.L.A.! After such treatment we are both seriously contemplating resigning from it.

Not all the Land Girls' complaints, however, were aimed at their employers. Some were directed at the W.L.A. organisation itself and included poor hostels, lack of adequate protective clothing for wet and cold work, and the unattractive uniforms. The Aertex blouses were described as 'dishcloths', hats as 'reminiscent of boarding school', the greatcoats as 'suitable only for maternity wear'. Even more heart-felt was the conviction that the W.L.A. was treated as an inferior organisation by the Government. Land Girls were not admitted to the canteen privileges shared by the W.R.N.S., A.T.S. and W.A.A.F. until August 1942 and even then were frequently not allowed to buy chocolates and cigarettes reserved for the forces. Some of the restrictions were downright petty, among them the order that from

Eleanor Roosevelt surrounded by Land Girls at Oldberrow Court Farm at Henley-in-Arden, Warwickshire.

Wearing large identification patches, Italian prisoners-of-war are marched off to do farm work in August 1941.

the summer of 1942 no more metal was to be issued for Land Girls' badges, although brass continued to be used in all other uniforms.

The worst example of discrimination came right at the end of the war when the Government excluded the W.L.A. from a service gratuity scheme and other demobilisation benefits. Lady Denman, the organisation's Honorary Director, resigned in protest in February 1945, but the Government remained adamant. All it could manage was a further £150,000 for the Womens' Land Army Benevolent Fund, free specialist training for those who wished to remain in agriculture after the war and retraining for those who did not. On top of this, members released after a minimum of six months' service were allowed to retain some items of uniform: the greatcoat dyed navy blue, one pair of shoes, a skirt and their badges. The concessions were described by Dame Edith Summerskill in the House of Commons as 'mean and niggardly'.

The Land Army reached its peak strength of over 87,000 in July 1943, shortly after which the Government was forced to suspend recruitment as more women were urgently required in the aircraft factories and munitions industries. In the later years of the war, farmers had to rely increasingly on prisoners of war and other casual workers.

The idea of using POWs was considered as early as 1940, but the difficulties of shipping them back from the Mediterranean meant that it was not until July 1941 that the first Italians began to turn up; some 2,400 had arrived in time to work on the harvest. Plans were drawn up to put another 28,000 to work. To begin with, the men were kept in camps and hostels, and went out to work in gangs under the control of armed soldiers, but from January 1942 'good conduct' prisoners were allowed to live on the farms.

Farmers still had to apply to the local War Ag for a prisoner and were expected to provide him with 'suitable accommodation, either in the farm house or in an outhouse, and food on the same scale as that provided for civilian workers.' Prisoners were not free labour: the War Ags were paid 40 shillings per week for each prisoner for the first three months and then 48 shillings, in both cases less 21 shillings a week board and lodging. The prisoner himself had to be paid six pence to a shilling a day, as laid down by the Geneva Convention. In spite of fears that farmers would not want prisoners in their homes, there was a great demand for Italians, who were seen as a much

45

better bet than Land Girls for heavy jobs such as beet lifting and ditching. Early reports suggested that their work was satisfactory, but there were also complaints from farmers who found the Italians too 'excitable' or 'born lazy'. Antony Hurd's opinion that 'they chatted when the sun shone but they were liable to get moody in the wet and rain' was considerably more charitable than the comments of the farm workers, who resented the fact that prisoners were often better fed and better equipped for bad weather, with rubber boots and capes. A Huntingdonshire labourer, Bill Petch, recalls:

They had army rations. The five or six Italians delegated one as cook and I have seen him throw more fat into the midday soup than my ration for a fortnight and they had a cooked meal before they came in the morning and another when the got back to the camp at night.

The prisoners would not work unless the farmers gave them cigarettes. The minimum amount was five each day. Few farmers admitted giving cigarettes but I believe they all did.

By July 1943, more than 37,000 POWs were working on the land, with a further 8,000 expected in time for the harvest. Even so, only about a thousand were billeted on the farms. The labour shortage became worse the following year and could no longer be alleviated by recruitment of more Land Girls, as the W.L.A. had reached its ceiling strength of 80,000. This meant that the Minister of Agriculture asked for 36,000 new prisoners to be made available for the 1944 harvest. The numbers were nearly reached, although some of the prisoners did not arrive until September, when the corn had already been cut.

An Italian prisoner-of-war shepherd takes his sheep to the free grazing ground on Cleeve Hill, near Cheltenham in Gloucestershire, in May 1945.

A farmer provides sandwiches for the Italian prisoners-of-war working on his farm in August 1941.

So far only Italians had been employed, but 1944 saw the use of Germans, at first on the potato harvest. According to one War Office official, there were still many 'dangerous fanatics' among the Germans, and careful selection was needed. At first they worked in strictly supervised gangs, but after a few months the regulations were relaxed and some of them were allowed to work in small groups without a guard. There was no question, though, of them living on the farms, nor were they to work alongside of the Italians for fear of trouble. Some farmers, who had reservations about the Italians, found the Germans more to their liking, and A.G. Street noted in *The Farmers Weekly* that 'from the little I have seen of the work of the German P.O.W. to date, he seems to be worth three average Italians; since the way in which many of the latter cycle and laze around the countryside is little short of offensive.'

A German refugee and an Italian prisoner-of-war bringing molasses for silage making on the Overbury Farms Estate in Worcestershire, June 1942.

The Pioneer Corps helps with stooking at Peacehaven in Sussex, August 1941.

Another group of people who were not working on the land from choice were the conscientious objectors. The tribunals which determined their fate could, between the extremes of over-ruling the objection and granting a complete exemption from war work, direct an objector either to non-combatant service in the forces or to a civilian occupation, notably agriculture. Thus Trevor Howard, now the rector of three country parishes on the border of Essex and Suffolk, was granted a exemption conditional first on his completing his studies at Cambridge and then on his taking up agricultural work. After two years working a 25-acre farm that he had bought at Dedham in Suffolk, he joined a community farming at Frating, near Colchester in Essex. There he worked with kindred souls, many but not most of them Quakers. Such communities tied in well with the pacifist ideal in trying to set up an alternative way of life based on co-operation. Perhaps, too, they were encouraged to group together through feelings of being outside a society that was dedicated to winning the war. Although most of the Frating community had little farming experience, they survived with the aid of injections of money from a wealthy member. Surprisingly, Trevor Howard and his companions were not cold-shouldered by the locals, most of whom would have had relatives in the forces, and the only expression of prejudice against them was the occasional remark.

Other helpers on the land were the casual workers, including the conscientious objectors who had not joined communities, as well as

Off-duty American soldiers join in the harvesting in August 1943.

48

Sailors at work in a Hampshire hayfield in July 1944.

internees, Irish migrants, the armed forces (not just British but also Polish, Canadian and American), schoolchildren, university students, and volunteers in their thousands from the women's organisations. and the cities. From 1941 onwards, the priority was to organise anyone who could be useful.

The farmers, who had been so reluctant to employ schoolchildren during their holidays in 1940, changed their minds by the following year, when over 12,000, organised in 335 camps, helped to bring in the harvest. Others went out from their own villages to help in the surrounding fields. The young excelled at the really back-breaking jobs, such as potato-picking and pea-pulling, at which they were invaluable during 'catchy' weather when speed was of the essence. According to Crichton Porteous, the Labour Officer of the Lancashire War Ag, boys in the county 'were weeding, hoeing, singling turnips, mangolds and beetroots, cabbage planting, picking strawberries and blackcurrants, hay making, corn harvesting, thistling, stone-picking, road making, silo-building and silage making . . . they were willing to tackle anything.' The girls helped too. According to a Lancashire farmer, Mr Heyes of Bickerstaffe, 'we farmers have said all sorts of things about unskilled labour, but the way some of these dainty High School girls have tackled the job out in the fields, seven and

E.A. Williams, himself a gipsy and a missionary welfare worker, recruiting other gipsies to work on the land.

49

eight hours a day, has fair capped me. You could not drive them back to camp.'

Under a Government order issued in May 1942, all children of twelve or over were allowed to work on the land at any time providing they did not miss more than twenty school attendances in a year. No child was allowed to work more than four hours in any half day, seven in a whole day or 36 in a week. They were to be suitably clad and shod, and arrangements were to be made for their transport to and from the farm. There was a statutory minimum rate of pay: boys of twelve to fourteen were to be paid 4d to 6d an hour, girls slightly less. The eight weeks of the school summer holidays were to be timed to suit agricultural needs.

The holiday labour camps which, until 1941, had been run by local and voluntary organisations were placed under a central committee representing the Ministry of Education, the head masters, the Ministry of Agriculture and the War Ags. With the improved organisation, some 654 camps were set up in 1942 and attended by 31,000 children, while in 1943 there were 105 camps and 63,000 thousand pairs of young hands helping with the harvest.

One of the camps was attended by Mr H.E. Bell, now Senior Assistant Registrar at Reading University. With other senior boys from High Storrs Grammar School for Boys, Sheffield, he found himself spending a fortnight of his summer holidays in 1942 and 1943 at a camp which had its headquarters in a substantial wooden building called the 'Old Isolation Hospital' at Walkeringham in Lincolnshire. The journey to the camp was meticulously organised. Before setting out by bicycle in a party of ten, each boy was required to give the master in charge a note certifying that he was free from infectious disease and that he had not recently been in contact with anyone with such a disease. The list of equipment to be brought was formidable:

Pair of boots for working in (football boots will do)
Pair of football stockings for working in
Pair of shorts
2 Pairs of socks
Pyjamas
2 Working shirts with open neck
2 Towels
Washing flannel and soap (no less than half a pound)

Felling and preparing pit props at a Youth Service Volunteer Camp near High Wycombe in Buckinghamshire, July 1944. Camps like this were for those between the ages of 15 and 20 who could not attend school camps and were too young for adult camps.

Toothbrush
Brush and comb
Boot polish and brush
Sweater or similar warm garment
Cape or light raincoat
Gas mask (no boy will be allowed to set off without one)
Ration card and points book. The former must be uncrossed for the two weeks you are spending at camp and the points book must contain 10 available points – no boy will be allowed to set off without these.
A pair of sheets (single bed size) or a sleeping bag – latter may be made from any suitable material
A spoon, fork, drinking mug and plate (knives and other plates will be provided)
Also, if possible, air-tight tin for sandwiches
And definitely lock for bike
Boys will therefore travel in their non-working garb, preferably grey flannels, school blazer and open neck cricket shirt. I am advised that the above equipment can be carried on a cycle, if suitable arrangements are made for strapping it on.

This holiday labour camp was very definitely not a holiday camp, with a timetable that went:

7 a.m. Reveille.
7.30 a.m. Inspection of dormitory and kit.
7.55 a.m. Prayers. Roll call.
8.00 a.m. Breakfast.
8.30 a.m. Distribution of lunches. Departure for farms.
7.30 p.m. Evening meal (this time may be altered according to circumstances).
9.30 p.m. Roll call.
10.15 p.m. Lights out.

One of young Ted Bell's letters home mentions the compensations for the hardness of the farm work:

The grub situation is excellent at camp – thanks largely to the two school cooks who lodge in the village and come over every day . . . to give you an example, last night we had roast pork, potatoes, cabbage, gravy and onion sauce – my plate was literally piled up to

Farmer Dan Crawford and his wife serving food to schoolboy potato pickers at Potterells Farm, North Mimms, Hertfordshire, in 1941. The food has been delivered by mobile canteen.

Public schoolboys at a camp at Overbury in Worcestershire trampling down layers of grass in silage-making, April 1943.

overflowing. For breakfast this morning we had toast and reconstituted egg (easily equals one egg) and tomatoes (i.e. after the excellent and inevitable porridge), bread and marmalade and tea. The helpings are liberal and often doubled. For lunch we got sandwiches filled with cheese and onions, fish (not paste – real fish), or something similar. The food situation at camp, albeit excellent and much superior to last year pales into insignificance beside the teas of jam or tomato sandwiches, the custards (real eggs!), the bakewell tarts, currant bread and buns we get on the farm, together with canful upon canful of lovely sweet, strong, milky tea, supplies of which come down to the field throughout the day.

For adults who responded to the call to 'lend a hand on the land', nearly every county had a register of country dwellers who could be mobilised at short notice. The East Suffolk War Ag had about 1,500 women in a scheme to help with fruit-picking and other work, while its equivalent in Warwickshire numbered some 3,000 women in its Emergency Land Corps. In Gloucestershire, the Women's Institutes took on the task of organising labour gangs for local women, and in East Sussex women between 14 and 60 who could not work on the land were asked to take over the household duties of those who could. Some of the volunteers recognised no age limit: in the village of Etton near Peterborough, Mrs Horner, a widow in her eighties, helped with the pea-pulling (and picked five bags a day); her two companions were both over 75.

Queen Mary, the Queen Mother, photographed with volunteer farmworkers during a visit to Wiltshire.

The Lend a Hand on the Land campaign. A cartoon in *The Farmer & Stock-breeder* in February 1943: 'People will go hungry unless they come and take off their coats.' A haystack in Trafalgar Square forms a recruiting office for Londoners signing on for voluntary work on the land.

Many townspeople, too, were also willing to give up evenings, week-ends or their annual holidays to help out on a farm. London had always provided a reservoir of casual labour for the surrounding countryside – hop-picking was a traditional Cockney activity – and by 1943 there were flourishing Land Clubs in such provincial centres as Hull, Salisbury, Shrewsbury and Northampton. Some organisations and businesses elected to adopt a farm by sending out a certain number of employees each week throughout the summer. Rather euphemistically this was represented as a holidays-with-pay scheme, but the results were remarkably good, with 20,000 volunteers at 160 adult camps in 25 counties. Between 70,000 and 80,000 more worked from their own homes.

All the efforts made 1943 a peak year for food production. A million acres of land were newly ploughed up and in spite of a good deal of rain in August and September, the production of wheat, barley and potatoes were all double the immediate pre-war average. The government resolved that the pressure should be kept up in 1944. Farmers were exhorted, as they had been the previous year, to 'take the plough around the farm' to find new land that could be taken into cultivation, while putting down worn-out arable land to

Pea-pulling in Kent in July 1944. Like hop-picking, this was a paid holiday for London families.

improved grass for grazing. But now the limit of expansion had been reached and the area under cereals decreased for the first time since 1939. The land had very nearly given its all, and in future greater allowance would have to be made for its recovery.

As always, much depended on the weather. In 1944, the spring was cold and dry – the pattern of the wartime years – and growth was held back. June was cold, with unseasonal storms, and July was no better. The beginning of August brought an improvement and the corn ripened at last so that cutting could start in the south and east. Then the weather turned wet and conditions remained unsettled

Gloucester shop assistants on their way to pick flax in August 1942.

Strawberry pickers at Kevington in Kent bring in baskets of fruit to be loaded, June 1942.

54

for the next two months. Much damage was done to the cereal crops, especially in the north of England and in Ireland. Because of this and the decreased acreage sown, the output of grain was down by ten per cent on the previous year. In the autumn, the lifting of the potato and sugar beet crops proved difficult and protracted. Not only was the potato crop light but its keeping quality was inferior, and in the spring of 1945 there was a potato shortage.

Although the spring of 1945 brought the end of hostilities in Europe, it did not result in any lessening of the struggle for food production. Foreseeing that, after the war, there would be rising demand for meat and dairy products and even greater shortages, the Ministry of Agriculture tried to stimulate livestock production by offering better prices as well as incentives for quality. Nonetheless, as the Nazi regime finally toppled, farmers could at least wipe some of the sweat from their brows and pause, however briefly, to take pride in their accomplishment. Addressing himself to the farming community as a whole, the Minister of Agriculture declared in May 1945, 'You have played an essential part in achieving victory and have every right to be proud of that.'

New land to plough up became harder to find and more difficult to deal with: gradients of one in three were among the problems in ploughing up part of Holcombe Moors, near Bolton in Lancashire, in February 1944 for reseeding as pasture.

The last 16 acres of a 900-acre deer park in Northamptonshire being cleared in June 1944 for food crops in a scheme that had started in the mid 'thirties.

The achievements of British agriculture had indeed been impressive. The output of wheat, barley, oats and potatoes had all virtually doubled, while at the same time the energy value of domestic food production rose by at least 90 per cent. This made the halving of food imports less disastrous and at the peak of the war effort released scarce shipping for vital purposes.

The increase in domestic production was gained only through enormous cost in terms of extra land and capital. Much of what was grown was not produced economically. After all, a philosophy of production at any cost was not compatible with one that put a premium on efficiency. The real significance of wartime agricultural policy, however, was that it both met the immediate need of filling stomachs and also forced the pace of modernisation with irreversible long-term consequences in British farming.

Greater reliance on fertilisers and machinery plus better management produced a massive increase in output with little extra labour. Between 1939 and 1946, the size of the tractor fleet had grown from 55,000 to over 200,000, and with the tractors came a greater range of implements, often with a much higher work capacity. The combine harvester, which cut, gathered and threshed the crop in one efficient operation, had been introduced into Britain in the late 1920s, but only a thousand were in use for the 1942 harvest; by 1944 there were 2,500. In spite of import restrictions, shortages of fuel and raw materials and the conversion of agricultural engineering factories into munitions works, the amount of mechnical power used on British farms grew by one and a half times during the course of the war.

By providing a wide range of technical and advisory services, the War Ags helped to raise standards in farming and instil a more open-minded approach to innovation. For example, their campaign against the reluctance of some farmers to buy artificial fertilisers more than doubled the amount of phosphates and more than tripled the amount of nitrogenous fertilisers being used. The basis of a post-war chemical and biological revolution in agriculture had been established.

Through subsidies and higher prices, the government offered substantial incentives to production, and agricultural prices rose by three times as much as the official cost of living index between 1939

Farm workers at Slade's farm, Bovey Tracey, Devon, being lowered from a hay rick which they have been making with a grab attached to a cable hauled by a horse, August 1945.

Bagging up potatoes from a clamp at Grange Farm, Weaverham, Cheshire, in March 1945.

Lawrence Smith, an 18-year old worker employed by the West Riding War Ag, claimant to a new record for tractor ploughing in April 1942. He turned over 50 acres of land (30 of them on a playing field at Bierley, near Bradford) in 75 hours.

Crocodile tears in a cartoon in *The Farmers Weekly* for 3rd March 1944: 'It's my conscience: I'm making far too much money . . .'

and 1945 while costs were strictly controlled. Particularly before 1942, the farmers found themselves with a generous income in place of pre-war unprofitability. Not all farmers benefited equally, and the importance attached to cereals meant that the arable farmers did best. This started the shift away from traditional mixed farming that has so changed the appearance of the rural landscape.

An unforeseen consequence of the war was that farmers became used to the idea of state direction and control. The War Ags, which represented both the farmers and the state, did much to establish a practical partnership which could continue after 1945. This set a pattern that was to survive for thirty years, with the farmers sacrificing some of their independence in return for the assurance of state aid and prosperity.

Apart from the stick of wartime regulations and the carrot of Government aid, there was an unbelievable amount of hard work behind the victory of British farming in World War II. Bill Petch, who worked as a labourer on a Huntingdonshire farm, recalls his work in the autumn of 1942:

I started work each morning at 05.00 . . . From then until nightfall, I kept going until I could hardly see the front of the tractor; after 20.30 I kept the engine running. I stopped only to refill with paraffin, to relieve myself, to swig tea from the bottle or to adjust the plough; I ate my sandwiches while ploughing.

So in about 14 hours ploughing time I ploughed ten acres, using 30 gallons of paraffin. I did this day after day, so, with only about 200 acres of autumn ploughing, it was finished in about three weeks.

It was above all in this spirit of just getting on with it that the battle for food was won.

Chapter 2
MAKING ENDS MEET

Food rationing was not introduced until early in 1940, although ration books, which had been printed before the war, were issued after National Registration Day on 29th September 1939. The delay was needed so that the administrative machinery could be set up: the rationing scheme was distinguished by the Government's guarantee always to honour ration coupons. To make sure this would happen, the Ministry of Food took on sweeping powers. It became the sole buyer and importer of all major foodstuffs, requisitioning existing stocks and imposing price controls on food marketed in the United Kingdom.

The first stage of rationing, on 8th January 1940, covered bacon and butter at 4 oz per person per week and sugar at 12 oz. On top of the basic ration, housewives making marmalade were allowed 3 lb of sugar and 2 lb of oranges, providing that their receipts for fruit were sent to the local Food Office. Beekeepers were provided for to the extent of 10 lb per colony between December and May.

Although Britain was one of the world's largest consumers of sugar, the rationing of butter, bacon and boiled ham was a greater blow to many families. As *The Field* commented just after the rationing had been announced, 'Bacon and butter are regular features of the Englishman's diet, and to all intents and purposes are permanent features of the nation's breakfast, which is, as everyone knows, essential to the Englishman's well-being.'

Meat rationing, which followed on 11th March 1940, worked on value – to begin with, 1s 10d per head per week. The cheaper the cut, the more you got – a couple choosing stewing steak could buy about 3 lb a week. Offal, and processed meats such as sausages, brawn, meat pies or meat pastes, were not rationed but there was no undertaking that they would be obtainable.

In July, rationing was extended to margarine and shortening, making a total fats allocation of 8 oz per person per week, in which the proportion of butter was progressively reduced until by October it stood at only 2 oz. Tea joined the list in the summer, but its importance to national morale was thought to be such that the new Minister of Food, Lord Woolton, insisted that a choice of blends should remain available in contrast to most products where a standard quality was introduced and even regional varieties were suppressed.

For eggs, milk and some vegetables the Government attempted to use other means of control by centralising distribution, removing competition and allocating supplies to shops in proportion to the number of registered customers. The result was virtually indistinguishable from rationing, except that supplies were not guaranteed. The solution to sharing out minor necessities was points rationing – originally a German idea – which was first applied to clothes in 1941. This valued each particular item at a certain number of points, and the ration book holder could purchase whatever he or she wanted up to a maximum number of points. This had the great advantage that simple adjustments could be made according to the level of

A Ministry of Food advertisement in *The Farmers Weekly* in June 1943 explains how to get new ration books. The reality shared by town and country alike: on the first day of rationing, 8th January 1940, a London housewife presents the family's ration books to get her ration of National Butter. Food supply in the country: selling eggs at the door at Aston in Oxfordshire, May 1941.

ISSUED BY THE **MF** MINISTRY OF FOOD

HOW TO GET YOUR NEW
RATION BOOKS

CUT THIS OUT FOR REFERENCE

1. See that the particulars on your identity card and food ration books (both buff and green) are correct, and that they *agree*. If these are not exactly the same, *do not alter them yourself*, but take both to your Food Office immediately.

2. Fill in page 3 of your present ration book (the Reference Leaf) including Section Z. But do not cut out this page.

GENERAL (Buff) BOOK

CHILD'S (Green) BOOK

3. On page 4 of the General (buff) Book (the back of the Reference Leaf), write the name and address of your present Milk retailer. On page 4 of the Child's (green) Book, write the names and addresses of the child's present Milk, Meat, and Eggs retailers. Never mind the printing; write on top of it. *Do not take out the page.*

4. Make sure that page 38 of your present ration book has been properly filled in.

5. Look out for A.B.C. posters like this in local cinemas, post offices, food offices, etc., and for advertisements in your local papers. Opposite your initial you will see where you should call and when. *The office will be situated in your own food control area.* It's no use going to any other place, or at any other time, than that shown on the poster or advertisements.

The new books and cards will be prepared and issued in alphabetical order of surnames. If there are different surnames in your household, it will mean more than one visit, but less waiting when you get there.

A friend can go for you, but *only* at the time, and place advertised for *your* surname.

6. Take your identity card and present ration book when you go for your new ones. You need not take personal points or clothing book. You will be given your new food ration book with personal points and clothing book (bound together but detachable) and, if you are over 16, a new identity card.

supplies, and anything that became scarce could have its points value raised, or lowered if it became plentiful. In November 1941, when the problem of shortages had become more serious, Lord Woolton brought in points rationing for canned meats and fish. The attack on Pearl Harbor led to the inclusion of other items which were expected to become much scarcer after the United States joined the war: pulses, canned fruit and vegetables, breakfast cereals, biscuits and condensed milk. The system worked well but did not guarantee that if you had enough points you would be able to buy what you wanted, as shopkeepers would reserve scarce points goods for their registered customers. Queues and under-the-counter sales were soon as common under points rationing as they had been before.

Rationing was the most visible aspect of the Government's food policy, but behind it was a determination that everyone should be adequately nourished. To put the national diet on as scientific a basis as possible, an eminent nutritionist, Professor J.C. Drummond, was appointed scientific adviser to the Ministry of Food in February 1940. Drummond stressed the importance of high quality bread, potatoes, oatmeal, cheese and green vegetables. The first report of the Scientific Food Committee in July 1940 proposed a largely vegetarian

Carroty George

He's a great favourite in the kitchen, our Carroty George. He has a hundred and one ways of making himself agreeable. Given a chance he'll enter into your pots and pans with real relish. Even if you reduce him to dice he won't be cut up ; and he takes frying, steaming, stewing or boiling, in perfectly good part. He plays the leading part in

Club Carrots

Scrub and grate 6 large carrots and mix with a teaspoonful of finely shredded white heart of cabbage. Make a dressing of 1 small teacupful thick unflavoured custard, 1 tablespoon salad oil, 1 teaspoon vinegar, ¼ teaspoon each mustard, pepper, and salt, and 1 tablespoon finely chopped pickles. Toast 4 thick slices of bread on each side, then slit open to make large pockets. Spread the insides of these pockets with margarine, and stuff with the filling. Serve at once. **A first-rate supper dish.**

MINISTRY OF FOOD

FOOD FACTS

The Scientific Adviser to the Ministry of Food sends you this message on how to keep well in the winter.

" I think you all know a little about protective foods by now. They're the foods that build you up and keep you merry and bright whatever infections may be about. You're going to need protection this winter, so I advise you all to eat plenty of green vegetables (especially watercress), carrots, potatoes, and salads.

Make sure of these protective foods and then you can eat what you like — and you should keep fighting fit."

Ministry of Food advertising promoted healthy eating and making the most of what was available, particularly vegetables. The recipes provided in a Food Facts for November 1940 and, with a little help from Walt Disney, in a Carroty George advertisement of January 1941, may look less than alluring from a viewpoint of peacetime plenty, but were a spirited effort at making an austerity diet seem less monotonous. The Ministry expressed its thanks to potato growers in *The Farmer & Stock-breeder* in February 1941.

Good News about Carrots

Here's good news! Carrots — one of the most valuable of all root vegetables — are plentiful this winter! Carrots are rich in Vitamin A which helps to protect us from many infections, including those of the throat and chest. We should serve them as often as we can. Here's one suggestion — braised carrots. Scrape 2 lb. carrots and slice them into rings. Heat 1 oz. fat in a saucepan, put in the carrots, cover, and cook for 10 minutes, shaking occasionally. Add 1 teacupful of stock or water with pepper and salt to taste. Cover the pan and simmer for ½ to ¾ hour. Dish up the carrots and keep them warm. Reduce the liquid in the pan a little by boiling; add a handful of finely chopped feathery carrot tops or some chopped parsley. Pour over the carrots and serve. Enough for four or five people.

Brose, a Scottish Recipe

This is another protective dish. Prepare and slice a turnip, a few carrots and some cabbage, or any other vegetables you have. Put them in a pan with a meaty bone, cover with water and simmer until tender.

Put a handful of oatmeal into a soup bowl (a separate bowl is required for each person), add a pinch of pepper and salt and a small piece of margarine. Now add a ladleful of stock from the pan while still boiling and stir. Serve immediately.

The vegetables themselves may be served for the next course.

A Winter Salad

This salad with wholemeal bread and butter (or margarine) makes a meal in itself. It is an excellent way of using up cooked meat.

Mix a teacupful of chopped cooked meat with four cooked potatoes, sliced thinly, and ½ a teacupful of cooked, diced carrots. Line a salad bowl with the finely sliced heart of a small raw cabbage and watercress sprigs, and pile the meat mixture in the middle. Round the pile arrange neat heaps of chopped celery and grated raw beetroot (you will need ½ a teacupful of each of these) and small bunches of watercress sprigs. Sprinkle a little chopped parsley over the middle pile and you will have a colourful and delicious dish. This serves four hungry people.

Cautionary Tale!

Auntie threw her rinds away.
To the lock-up she was taken.
There she is and there she'll stay
Till she learns to save her bacon!

Hear the answers to your food problems on the wireless at 8.15 every morning.

THE MINISTRY OF FOOD, LONDON, S.W.1

'siege diet' which could be supplemented with cheese, pulses, meat and fish, sugar and dried fruit to provide a 'production diet'. These ideas were unpopular with almost everyone, right up to Winston Churchill who considered the recommendations more appropriate to 'the downtrodden European peasantry than to the John Bull type of Englishmen'.

In fact, the siege diet was never forced upon the nation because livestock farming managed to keep going (albeit on a reduced scale) and the Royal Navy succeeded in keeping the Atlantic Corridor open, even during the darkest days of the war. The situation was also improved by developments in food technology: more meat could be imported if it came in as pressed, boneless carcases or processed in cans as Spam, Treet or Mor, and advances in dehydration allowed dried eggs, vegetables and fruit to be brought in. The Lend-Lease agreement with the United States, initiated in January 1941, was crucial in giving variety, taste and food value to the British wartime diet.

Under the guidance of Lord Woolton, the Ministry of Food, which had alienated the public in the first few months of the war by its distant and patronising attitude, started to improve its public relations. The Ministry published Food Facts in newspapers and periodicals, and put Kitchen Front broadcasts on the radio at 8.15 a.m. each day and Food Flashes on the cinema screen. These provided information on food prices and availability as well as help in making the most out of rationed food. A typical example of Food Facts might include instructions on how to cook fresh vegetables to retain their goodness ('Cabbage without Tears'), the best use of unfamiliar and dehydrated foods, notably dried egg powder, how to bottle fruit without sugar, and how to grow herbs for flavourings and tonics. A nationwide campaign was conducted to inform the public about nutrition and to publicise ration-stretching recipes. A wealth of advice, however, could not disguise the fact that the national diet was monotonous and often tasteless. Even the wartime banger, when it was available, was a poor imitation of the meaty pre-war sausage, and one of the Government's reasons for keeping the sauce and pickle industry going was to give flavour to otherwise dull food.

Although rationing was supposed to put everyone in the same boat, there were big differences between town and country eating. Townspeople envied country folk their fresh eggs, milk and vegetables, not to mention what they imagined to be a constant supply of poultry, mutton and home-cured bacon. Country people, on the other hand, also felt that they were missing out in some respects. They rarely had the opportunity to supplement their rations with restaurant meals (which were free of coupons) and frequently found that a consignment of off-the-ration goods in the nearest town had been snapped up by the locals before news of its arrival filtered out into the country. Petrol restrictions made shopping more difficult and time-consuming than before the war, with some shops, notably butchers, opening irregularly and roundsmen no longer calling.

Nevertheless, farming families did eat better than most. There was fresh meat to supplement the official ration: a family could kill one calf every three months and two pigs in a year. Farmers were

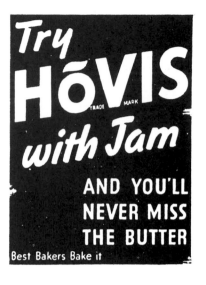

No coupons were needed for Pork & Leek Pie. HP Sauce, however, was essential.

The driver tells the farmer that he is asking too much for the run-over pig. 'Let's tune in to the Fat Stock Prices on my radio and see what he's worth.' A cartoon from *The Land Worker*, February 1940.

also allowed to slaughter a certain number of sheep for household consumption and to feed seasonal workers at busy times like shearing. Licences for slaughtering had to be obtained from the Local Food Executive Offices, but quite a lot of animals were killed unofficially, and casualties of Nazi air-raids were as likely to be dressed for the table as surrendered to the Ministry of Food. Farmers' wives were adept at using every part of the animal to eke out the meat supply as far as possible: prize-winning recipes published in *The Farmer & Stock-breeder* included Fried Bullock Brains, Fried Bacon with Dock Pudding, Sheep's Heart in Pastry and Stuffed Pig's Trotters, as well as this recipe for Lambs's Tail Brawn:

Simmer the tails gently till meat comes away from bone, using only enough water to cover. Drain, remove bones, return to pan with liquid and salt and pepper to taste. Bring to the boil. Into a basin put alternately a layer of meat and a layer of boiled egg cut in rings until the basin or bowl is full. Leave to stand until cold, then turn out.

To clean lamb's tails, keep the saucepan of water boiling and put a few tails into it at a time. Lift out one tail with a fork and if the wool will pluck off clean, put the tail at once in a bowl of cold water and finish cleaning when all the tails have been dealt with in the same manner. Rub them dry in a cloth and singe thoroughly. Wash in salt water, drain and dry, and they are ready for cooking.

Any traditional mixed or dairy farm yielded a plentiful supply of milk, which was used for butter or cheese making as well as for a variety of puddings. Then there would usually be fresh eggs, perhaps home-baked bread and home-made jams or preserves. Greater self-sufficiency during war made extra work, which the farmers' wives seemed to take in their stride. One wrote to *The Farmers Weekly* in June 1944:

Apart from the rations and cocoa, coffee, custard powder and points foods like biscuits occasionally, crushed oats, syrup, dried fruit, and herrings or pilchards, we produce the rest of our food at home . . .

The bees are very little trouble – a Sunday afternoon job; and everybody helps with extracting the honey! The poultry, except for the hatching and rearing, only take about fifteen minutes a day; apart from the regular clean-out.

Ducks and geese feed themselves all the summer. With tail corn, home grown oats, chat potatoes and mangolds, we need buy little feed; I keep up the protein with dried yeast (off the ration) and fish meal.

The pigs are even less trouble. I keep a tame breeding sow, and fatten two of her litter for bacon. Killing a pig means a little work for a few days – making faggots and brawn, rendering down fat, salting bacon – but it is well worth it when the meat ration runs out (as it usually does by the middle of the week).

Mrs Joan Blackmore was equally able to cope. She was just 21 in 1940 when her mother died and she took over running the farmhouse on a mixed farm in Cornwall. She remembers that rationing had just begun to take effect, but the farm provided for most needs:

I had a hundred Rhode Island Reds and crossed them with White Wyandottes or those fighting, good laying, skinny White Leghorns, as well as a number of Khaki Campbell and Aylesbury Ducks – so we had an abundance of eggs and roosters and boilers. The egg money was my special perk, as no wages came my way. We killed a fat pig once a year at least; now and again we shared it with neighbouring farmers, when their turns came round we were remembered.

We cured hams and bacon – I have no idea how I knew what to do – and of course the usual jam making etc. was normal. One of the greatest helps came during threshing time. We could apply to the Ministry of Food for extra sugar, tea, dried fruit, canned meat and coal, because in those days we still had visiting gangs of thresher-men. There was a huge steam traction engine, pulling a threshing machine, with usually three men in charge, I believe – the driver and two helpers. There were other casual labourers and our own farm labourers. They were big, grimy-faced shy men who would come at 5.30 a.m. to stoke the boiler and get up steam, and then come into the farm kitchen expecting vast plates of bacon, eggs, sausages (or Cornish hog's pudding), fried bread and plates of bread and butter (I made the butter too!), and tea of great strength and thickness. The whole gang expected a big basket of 'croust' which is Cornish for elevenses. I made batches of saffron buns and cakes (until saffron became unobtainable), or white yeast cake with currants or sultanas (as the war went on these became fewer and fewer – sometimes dried prunes and dates helped), or heavy cake (like scones but cut in squares and not light and airy; with dried fruit, it was very sustaining).

I also made kettles of cocoa, hot and sweet and milky. I don't remember being short of cocoa, which seems strange when choc-olate and sweets were rationed. At midday we sent out kettles of tea and fed the three threshing men only, usually with big Cornish pasties, which they preferred, otherwise they had to come indoors for a sit-down meal. I think they expected some kind of pudding which was often some sort of sweet cake or apple pies. The after-noon break was simpler with only tea and maybe sandwiches or biscuits as a rule. I think the machine men went after dowsing down the steam engine and making all ready for the next day's work . . . I stress these 'threshing' days because the extra rations made such a difference – if we filled our forms in for the extra amounts needed, they were usually cut in half, or at least reduced. We always asked for more than we needed – and just gained a little. We knew nothing of the 'black market' as such – but for self preservation we cheated a little!

Farm workers usually did not do so well. One complaint from the winter of 1940 was the shortage of cheese, which was eaten with bread at two meals a day – lunch at 9.30 or 10 o'clock and dinner at 12 or 1 o'clock. Few dairy farmers continued to make their own cheese, and even factory-produced cheese was reduced in quantity as more milk was diverted into the liquid market. A certain amount was imported from Australia, but by the spring of 1941 many farm workers were having to make do with a little jam instead, which 'don't fill your belly when you are out in the air all day.' *The Farmers Weekly* interviewed a number of the labourers in March:

No one would talk anything but cheese; it is only cheese that mat-ters to them. Meat, sugar, bacon and ham and other commodities in short supply do not worry them greatly – it is just cheese for which they are pleading.

Every man tells practically the same story. 'I have always had cheese . . . It has always been our main food . . . Nothing can take its place.'

They grin when jam is mentioned. Very few care for it and if they do they cannot get enough. It is the same with potted meat and various fish pastes.

Fat bacon would help in place of cheese but that's off the menu and very few folk in small country villages can get sausages.

So they are just eating bread and margarine (they leave the butter

A market gardener at Cheltenham in Gloucestershire solves the labour shortage by inviting the public to pick their own raspberries. 500 people arrive within an hour of his announcement and clear the day's crop – a reason, notes *The Farmers Weekly* in August 1941, why there is so little fruit to be had in the larger towns.

ration for the youngsters). Sometimes there is a bit of dripping – depends on the week-end joint – and now and again a bit of lard.

Some of them are very disgruntled. They know there is cheese about, 'in restaurants, where people do not really need it because they could buy something else.' And in the Army where they allege it is often wasted. Said one man: 'We had some soldiers camping near here. They were being given such quantities of cheese that they were fed up with it and much was thrown away – wasted.'

Shortly after this, the Ministry of Food relented, and farm workers were given an allowance of 8 oz of cheese per week. This was later raised to 12 oz, compared with an ordinary ration of 1 oz to 3 oz per person per week. Even such a limited extra ration annoyed some townspeople who argued, like Mr S.O. Rowe, that 'plenty of city dwellers have heavier work under more arduous and perilous conditions than the agricultural workers, and there is no reason why they should sacrifice a proportion of their rations to satisfy the noisy clamour of one section of the community.' The publication of such a comment in *The Farmer & Stock-breeder* in April 1941 provoked enraged replies from countrymen. In the course of a massive fulmination, Viscount Monck took up another point:

Mr S.O. Rowe states that 'practically the whole of the community other than the agricultural folk have had to alter their lives and circumstances.' I hesitate to guess Mr. S.O. Rowe's occupation in life, but merely wonder whether he falls into the category of those whose working day in London was conveniently pruned during the last winter in order to enable them to reach home before the black-out.

Whether or not he is directly concerned, it is a fact that thousands of city workers have benefited from this concession, while the farm worker has seen not only his hours of labour increased but also his routine completely altered in order to assure that starvation will not be the lot of his fellow men, including Mr. S.O. Rowe . . .

The Ministry was trying to provide even-handedly for every part of the population, but Lord Woolton's decision to increase rations for medium and heavy industrial workers via works canteens renewed controversy. Few farms had canteens, and the scattered nature of farming made it unlikely that many workers could take advantage of such facilities. Nevertheless, various initiatives were tried. British Rural Restaurants, akin to the British Restaurants

Lunch-time in the fields on a farm in the West Riding of Yorkshire, April 1944.

which provided food at low prices in the towns, were very successful where they were established, but they could cater only for the workers and their families who could get to them easily. Farm canteens had much the same problem, but a number were established on estates where the work force was large enough. On his 79th birthday, David Lloyd George, who had been Prime Minister during World War I, opened a canteen on his estate at Churt in Surrey. The occasion was reported in *The Farmer & Stock-breeder* on 20th January 1942:

A long wooden building, formerly used as a fertiliser store, had been converted by the farm carpenter into a canteen and recreation room, and the food on Saturday, cooked in the new British Restaurant at Haslemere, arrived steaming hot in one of the emergency food supply vans presented by Mr. Henry Ford and his son Edsel.

Judging by the reception given by the sixty or so workers who enjoyed the meal, the experiment will be a big success. The 7d course included Cornish pasty and potatoes, carrots and other vegetables; the sweet (raisin pudding) cost 2d, and cups of tea 1d each. On this first occasion Mr. Lloyd George was host, he had provided additional refreshments.

Earlier, Major Gwilym Lloyd George, MP, had opened the new British Restaurant (which is combined with the Rural Cash and Carry Service) in Haslemere. Distribution to the farms will be carried out by members of the Women's Voluntary Service.

At Bron-y-dee Farm, Mr. D.C. Withers, farm agent, thanked Mr. Lloyd George on behalf of the workers for providing the canteen and recreation room, and gave the toast 'Good health and many happy returns of the day to Mr. Lloyd George, our master.'

Hatfield Rural Council in Hertfordshire pioneered the idea of using a mobile canteen to take food out to the men in the fields in October

1941. Hot midday meals were cooked in a Salvation Army kitchen in the town and then taken to the fields in metal containers by the W.V.S. using a vehicle donated by the American Red Cross. The Ministry of Food encouraged other councils to follow Hatfield's example, but many were deterred by the general petrol shortage and the problems of keeping the food hot.

More practical was the rural meat pie scheme. The W.V.S., Women's Institutes and other voluntary groups were approached by the local War Ags to distribute meat snacks to men where they worked. The village baker would bake them, and about a pennyworth of meat per head was allowed, although other fillings and sandwiches might be substituted. The scheme expanded rapidly in 1942 and 1943, at its peak selling something like a million and a half pies a week. Demand fell towards the end of the war – in the Brigg District of North Lincolnshire, it had slumped from 6,000 to 2,000 pies a week by the beginning of 1945.

Apart from the various substitutes for factory canteen meals, agricultural workers were supposed to receive extra rations at peak times such as harvest, lambing, sheep shearing and potato lifting. They did not always receive them because it was the farmers' responsibility to apply for and distribute them. Many farmers could not be bothered to fill in the forms or, if they did, failed to give out the rations fairly or at all. Bill Petch recalls that, on the Huntingdonshire farm where he worked, the farmer would use the additional allowances to feed the paying guests he took in from the bombed cities. 'Farm workers,' said the National Union of Agricultural Workers, 'cannot understand why they are not allowed to apply to Food Offices as individuals for extra ration permits as they have done with cheese. They feel that the Ministry does not trust them.' The Union also repudiated the view, which it thought was held by the Ministry as well as by the public, that farm workers got perks such as chickens, rabbits and eggs from their employers, pointing out that 'farmers get such favourable prices for poultry etc. these days, that workers get little of them.'

For whatever reason, the Ministry stuck to its policy of issuing rations in bulk to farmers. However, it did sanction small increases

The W.V.S. rural meat-pie scheme in operation near Reading in Berkshire, July 1942.

Members of a food production club in the Home Counties draw their seed potatoes for planting in May 1942. Utilising derelict land in the district, some hundreds of locals grew potatoes and fed pigs, poultry and rabbits on the throwouts.

in farm workers' rations: by the spring of 1945, each worker received an extra ⅘ oz of tea, 1 oz of sugar and half a pint of milk per week, with seasonal allowances of ¼ oz tea, ⅘ oz sugar, ¾ oz margarine, ⅖ oz cheese, ¾ oz preserves and half a ration point per day. Where there was no provision for adequate packed meals, farmers could also get enough supplies to give each man two snack meals per day.

One way for farm workers to supplement their diet was setting up a pig club. The Government was keen to encourage new clubs so long as the animals could be fed mainly on edible waste, and the first three years of war saw more than 3,400 new clubs registered with the Small Pig Keepers Council. Frank Swanton, whose five farms at Overton and Fyfield (in Hampshire) covered 4,000 acres of down and valley, gave the 69 members of the local pig club the use of one of his pig houses and sold them a number of Large White/Saddleback crosses. The club members collected swill from the local villagers and this, mixed with a little meal ration, allowed them to fatten 158 pigs in their first year. Half were sold to the Ministry of Food (one pig had to be sold for every one eaten) and each household ended up with about 3 lb of bacon a week and a small contribution to its income.

The money was always welcome as making ends meet was a struggle for many labourers' wives. Even skilled workers brought home a modest wage packet, which would only just cover the necessities of life, as is shown in this letter published in *The Farmers Weekly* on 23rd June 1944:

I am the wife of a tractor driver in Berkshire. Our wage is £3 10s per week, clear of insurance. We have no rent or rates to pay. Two pints of milk daily, and what wood we like to bring in, are free. In addition to myself and my husband, our family consists of two little boys of four and nearly six, the latter just started at school but not having his dinner there.

Our cottage is sound and well-built, but has no services except main water, so our cooking and lighting expenses go in coal, paraffin and candles. This is how the weekly budget works out. I put regular commitments first.

Food rations for four, including meat, fats, cheese, tea, sugar, bacon: 10s 6d; points goods, jams, other groceries, soaps, polishes, etc., 10s; baker (five to six loaves weekly, also 3 lbs of flour, sometimes yeast): 3s; paraffin: 2s 3d; coal: 3s 6d; greengrocer (average through year, including fruit for jam and bottling in the season, some potatoes and other vegetables when our own run short): 2s; newspapers: 1s 9d; agricultural pies (we have these because they are sent to the farm and come in handy at times, but we don't really think they are worth the money or a good addition to the family rations): 2s 4d.

Pint of milk daily (in addition to our free quart – it is charged 4d a pint): 1s; savings stamps (one each for children): 1s; postage stamps, etc.: 1s; tobacco (3 oz at 2s 4d): 7s; laundry (I wash most things myself, but send sheets and big things and oily overalls): 1s 4d; children's sweets (3 quarters of a pound weekly at 6d per quarter): 1s 6d; balance of meal for hens: 1s; children's orange juice and cod liver oil (1s 8d a month at Food Office): 5d; hospital scheme (this has proved its worth twice in the last couple of years): 4d. This adds up to £2 11s 9d.

We are left with 18s 3d weekly for the variable expenses – boot repairs, fares, new bicycle tyres and parts (as we live nearly two miles from any bus, three from the nearest shop and five from town you can guess these items are bound to mount up. If it isn't one, it's another!).

In our garden we grow a lot of vegetables; so seeds, tools, fertilisers, etc. are a big item in their season. As for clothes – well, we manage on as few as possible; when I say that last year's ration books are still intact, no clothing coupons gone at all, you will see that I do a lot of mending of other people's cast offs instead!

We scarcely ever go to the theatre or cinema, and my husband, though enjoying a pipe, does not drink. Yet it is pretty hard to keep the budget balanced, and if we had 12s 6d cottage rent to pay, we definitely could not balance it.

I ought to mention that my husband has life and fire insurance policies that swallow up getting on £4 1s a week; which we reckon to pay out of overtime, or odd jobs that I can do.

Where the wage-earner was drafted into the forces, rural life could be even harsher, although sharing between neighbours helped. One young girl and her brother were brought up by their grandmother after the father was called up and the mother went to work in a furniture factory in High Wycombe, which had gone over to making parts for aircraft. She remembers:

We grew up on a diet of vegetables and pancakes that were made of flour and water and fried. Sheeps' heads made a stew most days because sheeps' heads and pigs' heads were off ration. We were allowed 2 oz of corned beef a week and 2 oz butter. We had dried milk and dried eggs but I don't remember having sugar all the wartime. We ate dandelion leaves for salads; stinging nettles for cabbage, hawthorn leaves, raw turnips and carrots. Wild raspberries, strawberries, blackberries were collected by us children.

Everything was shared much more than it is today. We borrowed clothes from each other, or tea cloths and extra china when there was a birthday to celebrate. I broke the only tea pot we had; there was no getting another one, such things were not in the shops. We made tea in the kettle after that.

We had to have coupons for food and clothes, so a good many things were made out of parachute silk or old wool pulled out and reknitted. Coal was very short, my aunt used to travel from Nottingham by train to see us and would bring down a suitcase full of coal. Her son was a miner!

Gran used to collect all the horse manure she could for her garden as there were more horses about and not many cars. Gran sold the flowers she grew for the Red Cross; we children put on small plays to collect money for the Red Cross. We also knitted scarves for the troops in khaki wool. When we went out to play, we played hop scotch or skipped or paddled in the river close by. There were very few toys then.

The combination of rising prices and scarcity meant a generally lower standard of living, although some country dwellers were stimulated to greater efficiency and adaptability. For thrifty housewives, it was a time of 'making do' or 'stint and wangle'. This was nowhere more evident than with clothes. When points rationing was introduced in the summer of 1941, a high coupon value was set on all woollen items, ranging from overcoats and suits to underwear, as the services had first call on wool imports. From its patrician viewpoint, *The Country Life* commented that 'to be out at elbows was once a mark of amiable eccentricity, now it will be that of patriotism.' Country housewives, however, saw clothes rationing as a challenge to their skills with the needle. Mrs Blackmore recalls:

Farmers' market best clothes lasted for ever, being bought of good quality always. Otherwise we all learned to make and mend, unpicking, dyeing and reknitting all kinds of woollies, repairing suits and shirts, making one dress out of two and adapting evening dresses. I became a great mender and patcher. My third brother, who posted home all his personal laundry to me to wash, iron and mend, did plead at one time for some coupons for new shirts as all his shirts were without tails and on one he had counted fourteen patches.

Those working on farms were helped by being given supplementary clothing coupons for oilskins, rubber boots and other protective clothes, and in the latter part of the war reconditioned battledress provided men with useful working garb at reasonable prices. Land Girls were not so lucky, as their uniform, though warm and comfortable, was inadequate in really harsh or wet weather. There were long delays in the arrival of the necessary oilskins and rubber boots. The editor of *The Farmers Weekly* took up their cause in October 1942: 'If a Land Girl is not protected from drenching rain and the quagmire underfoot sooner or later she has to leave her work – at least until she dries out. She becomes, in a word, a casualty. What sort of an Army is it that makes casualties of its own?' Later he returned to the attack:

About the gum boot question. Gum boots seem to go in healthy quantities to R.A.F. personnel. Not that I grudge them anything. But I very much doubt if they need them all.

Is there any reason why these boots should not be issued only at stations where mud is deep and affectionate instead of handing them out to all and sundry at the Recruiting Centre?

No redistribution of waterproofs in the direction of the W.L.A. was ever managed, and the grievance remained until the end of the war.

For women generally, clothes rationing spelt the end of fashionable changes of wardrobe and, in the words of one squire's lady, of 'shopping expeditions for flimsy stockings and fal-lals.' She added regretfully, 'One cannot do as one has always done, buy a new spring

Advertisement in *The Farmers Weekly*, July 1941.

'COUPONOMISE'
at *Pontings*
SALE

Bigger value per coupon means greater economy

Rayon Spun FROCK

19/F.W.40.—Heavy quality smart and becoming style Gold, Saxe, Grey, Rose, with contrast design.
Post 5d. Price **12'11**
Lengths ... 44, 44, 45 in.
Hips ... 40, 42, 44 in.
5 Coupons.

Printed Rayon Spun Frock

47/F.W.79.—With swing skirt, self Robespierre collar, and buttoning to waist. In floral Rayon Spun Predominating colours of Saxe, Rust, Green, Cherry, Clover, and Fuchsia. Give second choice of colour. Price **10'9**
Post 5d.
Lengths ... 40, 41, 42, 43 in.
Hips ... 38, 40, 42, 44 in.
5 Coupons only.

OUTSIZE TWO-PIECE

66/F.W.109.—Full-length plain Marocain Coat with patterned Spun Rayon Frock. Black, Navy, Brown, Lido.
(Give second choice.)
Post free. Price **35'9**
10 Coupons.
Lengths ... 50, 50, 50, 52 in.
Hips ... 48, 50, 52, 54 in.

Lightweight MACS

46/F.W.206.—(a) Single-breasted, unbelted stroller (as sketch), or (b) double-breasted, belted, with storm collar. Good rubber-proofed Indiana. Off White, Light or Dark Fawn, Nigger, or Green. Stock sizes lengths 40, 42, 44, 46 in.
9 Coupons
Post 7d. Price **15'9**
Outsizes 18/9. (Single-breasted Style only)
Lengths ... 40, 42, 44, 46 in.
Bust ... 40, 40, 42, 44 in.
Lengths ... 42, 44, 46, 48 in.

Man-Tailored SKIRT

45/F.W.13.—Inverted pleat back and front. Soft finish, hard-wearing cloth. Black, Navy, Brown, Wine, Bottle.
Post 7d. Price **12'11**
Lengths 26, 27, 29 in.
Hips ... 36, 38, 40 in.
7 Coupons.

Pure Wool SKIRT

45/F.W.11.—Well-cut Skirt, made in good quality flecked plain and all-wool Oatmeal Cloth.
Post 7d. Price **14'11**
Lengths ... 26, 27, 29, 30 in.
Hips ... 36, 38, 40, 42 in.
7 Coupons.

'Spunshine' Frock

19/F.W.49.—In gay print effect. White collar, built-up shoulders, straight youthful front, and half-belt to tie up at back. Multi light shades of Saxe, Gold, Green, and Helio. (*Please give second choice of colour.*)
Post 5d. Price **12'11**
Lengths ... 40, 42, 44 in.
Hips ... 40, 42, 44 in.
5 Coupons only.

Rayon Spun FROCK

47/F.W.73.—Predominating shades of Saxe, Brown, Rust, Cherry, Green, Clover, and Lilac. Give second choice.
Price **10/-**
Lengths ... 40, 42, 44, 44 in.
Hips ... 38, 40, 42, 44 in.
5 Coupons only.

PONTINGS *The House for Value* **KENSINGTON, W.8** **WEStern 7272**

hat – the latest from Paris – and let them post the old one home.'

1942 brought utility clothing in officially approved designs which allowed some scope for individuality of style but were mainly notable for their practicality and economy in the use of material. *The Farmer & Stock-breeder* offered fashion notes in March 1944 on a parade of utility wear in a big London store:

While there are no very drastic changes in fashion to be noted, novelty and variety have been preserved by means of unusual pockets, buttons, and so forth. Many of the frocks, in rayon and other lightweight materials, are in dainty pastel shades; some are in two-colour combinations, such as blue and brown, red and white, green and tan, two shades of blues.

Suits, so practical for both town and country wear, are in tweeds, pinstripe and plain materials. The coats are rather longer but closely fitting, while the skirts mostly have two or three box-pleats. Full-length coats are semi-fitting with novel pockets and high revers and are available in navy, black, off-white, and various colours. The 'outsize woman' has not been forgotten and she has a choice of becoming dresses and coats specially designed to meet her needs.

As to prices – nothing the display referred to cost more than 94s

4d, which was the price for the navy and black full-length coats for the older woman. Other coats and suits were priced at from 80s to 92s 10d. Frocks were round about 50s to 60s; and a long-sleeve lemon yellow blouse, designed for wear with a black skirt, cost 19s 3d.

Country women were driven to the same ruses as their urban sisters to deal with the lack of anything that the Government did not consider absolutely necessary, for example, overcoming the shortage of nylons by applying make-up to their legs or getting a friend to draw a dark line down the back of the leg to disguise the bare skin. Parachute silk was greatly in demand for making slips and perhaps French knickers. Existing garments had to be cosseted, and K.M. Chapple had some advice in June 1943 for readers of *The Farmer & Stock-breeder* on the best way of washing corsets:

If you can get a little starch to stiffen the corsets when washing them so much the better. First take out all the steels. Make a lather of soap and warm water, then swish the garments round and round in it until fairly clean. Squeeze, and take out of water. Prepare more lather and add 1 oz of cream of tartar. Leave the corsets in this for a quarter of an hour. Take out, lay on a board, and brush all over with a nail brush or other small but fairly stiff brush.

The garment should now look perfectly fresh and clean. Hang to dry on an outdoor line in a strong current of air. Rapid drying is important for good results.

As the war went on, the supply of soaps and soap powders began to dry up. One useful trick was to save small scraps of soap and melt them down into a soap jelly by pouring a little boiling water over them and adding a teaspoonful of borax to every pint of the solution. Borax could also be added to the weekly laundry to loosen the grease and dirt and soften the water so that less soap was required to make a good lather. From March 1942, an extra allowance of 'farm soap' could be obtained by going to the local Food Control Office with form Soap 1. In spite of the shortage, some companies continued to advertise their product, taking care to sound a patriotic note:

Victory is bound to be ours. Support Britain. Buy an unequalled deodorant, healthy, antiseptic Carbolic Soap – PETOBOLIC. Present conditions make it difficult for us to supply everybody – but be certain to buy truly BRITISH soap – your money then remains in OUR country.

By the middle of the war, countless personal and household items became virtually unobtainable, and small necessities had turned into prized luxuries. Men found the scarcity of razor blades particularly vexing and many invented their own ways of keeping blades sharp. Some thought that careful drying and smearing with vaseline was enough, but others found it necessary to rub the blade against glass or emery paper. Devotees of the cut-throat razor had an easier time, though not all equalled the performance of Colonel Hardcastle's blades, about which he wrote to *The Field* in October 1943:

Sir: – Mr. Moffat again refers to this interesting question and believe it or not, I have used a single blade every day for 21 years, and thereby hangs a tale. I was returning from the Boer War, on completing my term of service with the Imperial Yeomanry and had got down to Port Elizabeth from Graaf Rennet.

I went on into the town to have my hair cut. My barber, like most, had much to say. At last he pointed with pride to a strap hanging on the wall and went on to explain that it was made from leather taken from the neck of a zebra. 'I would not take £5 for it,' he said, but when I produced a 5-pound note, I secured the cheapest bargain I ever made. I started to use it at once and for 21 years it put a perfect edge on my single blade and I might be using it still if I had not dropped the blade on to the fender in my room and chipped a bit out of it, making it useless. That was in 1922. I then purchased a Wilkinson set of 3 blades in a case. They keep just as keen an edge as the single one and I get a perfect shave each morning. Why the leather from a zebra's mane should have this extraordinary property in keeping a blade in such perfect condition I do not know. I occasionally put some oil on the back.

Yours faithfully,
Henry M. Hardcastle
Colonel
Bradshaw Hill,
Bolton,
Lancs.

People habitually went to what now seem extraordinary lengths to make things last or recycle the bits that were not worn out or used up. Peggy Fraser had several useful tips for readers of *The Farmer & Stock-breeder* in April 1941:

Save all spent matches and put them into old matchboxes or cigarette boxes. Several of these are helpful in lighting the fire.

Save two or three medium-sized cinders from those that are to be put at the back of today's fire, soak them in a tin containing a little paraffin, and use them to-morrow as fire lighters. They will definitely save wood.

Use coal dust mixed with damp tea-leaves and packed into discarded cartons or small discarded meal bags to keep the fire going steadily without waste while you are out.

A scrap metal salvage team from the Ministry of Works using a motor-roller to flatten tin cans, old kettles and other scrap collected in a salvage drive in Hertfordshire, April 1943.

Repairing hop sacks used by Whitbreads brewery, which until 1940 had not found it worthwhile to mend and re-use damaged sacks.

Save that discarded kid glove, cut off the unworn fingers and keep them wrapped up in your medicine chest. One day a finger-stall will be needed in a hurry. Cut strips from the good parts of the rest of the glove and use double as small window wedges on windy nights.

Stick a metal knife sharpener or old penknife into a candle-end, heat the candle slightly and rub it quickly all over the sole of leather shoes you wear when going out into rain or snow. You will make the leather waterproof, use up a candle-end, and probably save yourself from catching cold from damp feet.

Save empty cotton reels and use them, preferably painted or stained, as door stoppers, just behind those doors in the house that otherwise are banged back against the wall, causing damage to the wallpaper. A long screw right through the cotton reel and into the floor woodwork keeps the door-stopper firm.

Save furniture and floor polish by lavishly sprinkling the cloths with which they are to be applied with paraffin. The paraffin will prevent the polishing cream soaking into the cloths.

Furniture was well worth looking after, as timber was scarce and its use was strictly controlled. Utility furniture arrived before utility clothing, in January 1941, with the introduction of Standard Emergency Furniture made to stringent specifications and stamped with the ubiquitous CC41 Utility mark. Cheap, serviceable and, within its limits, well-made, it was eagerly sought by young families setting up their home. The better-off, though, scorned what they saw as its orange-box construction and tried to preserve their solid pre-war pieces.

The efforts that went into saving and recycling every conceivable type of industrial and domestic junk would impress even the most thorough-going of today's conservationists. Scrap metal was required for making shells, tanks and aircraft, not to mention tin cans and even new agricultural implements. Waste paper could be turned into components for munitions and radio sets as well as army boot stiffeners and wall board for service huts. Animal bones could be purified and melted down to make glues used in aircraft and other industries; they also yielded fertilisers and gelatine for making sweets, jams and photographic film. Such rubbish as could not be recycled went into the furnaces of the salvage plant to provide steam power, leaving a residue of clinker for making roads, runways and building blocks.

Council scrap metal dump at Dartford in Kent, June 1940.

The drive to collect old iron and steel from rural districts started in earnest in the early summer of 1940. As scrap merchants were unlikely to make rounds outside the towns, villagers were asked to organise their own 'comb-out' and make dumps that would be periodically cleared. Hedgerows and neglected undergrowth in farmyards gave forth a rich harvest of obsolete machinery. A farmer who went through the local village collecting scrap metal ended up with his horse-drawn wagon 'piled high with bits of old bedsteads, at least three old ovens, quite a lot of massive cracked iron pots, grates, old spades and broken digging forks, old window bars, weights from window sashes, solid hefty rusty hooks on which the family pig used to be suspended in days gone by, bits of bicycles, old iron guttering, bent pokers, flat-irons and old buckets.'

Children were frequently co-opted into their village's effort to collect scrap, organised perhaps by the vicar or the local educational authority. In Copdock, East Suffolk, it was a small group of boys and girls who took the initiative, borrowing a horse and cart from a neighbouring farmer and collecting two complete cart loads from twelve houses. The example caught on, and within a month during the late summer of 1940 over a hundred squads were at work in East Suffolk. The squads, which varied from five to six in isolated villages to thirty or forty in larger places, not only produced quantities of metal and paper, but went on to collect vegetables for minesweepers and funds for the local War Savings Committees.

A less admirable way of overcoming shortages was the Black Market. It is difficult to establish how widespread it was, but *The Field* saw it in March 1942 very much as organised crime:

A year ago Lord Woolton, Minister of Food, made a speech in which he promised that the Black Market would be driven out of business. In the intervening period the Black Market has grown from a small individual 'racket' into an enormous highly-efficient and totally unscrupulous organisation. Now Parliament has discussed repressive measures. So much for speeches.

Lord Woolton, one of the very few men whose Ministry has been a success, undoubtedly did his best. The Ministry of Food undertook a vast number of prosecutions, but fines mean nothing to gentry who are making enormous profits. Furthermore, these prosecutions touched only the fringe of the market. All these men with the interesting names who have been fined, and in a few cases sentenced to a month or so in prison, are the servants. The big men in the business have not been touched and the big men do not object to fines at all and are not moved by prison sentences that do not touch them personally. Make no mistake about it. There are big men at the back of the Black Market; there is a big distributive organisation; there is a big warehousing organisation; there is a highly effective intelligence service. The Black Market is not made up of a large number of individuals acting independently, but a large number of individuals well organised. The thefts are on too large a scale for it to be otherwise. You cannot store 40 thousand eggs nor 5 tons of meat on the kitchen shelves. And these quantities are not easy to distribute.

While such organised racketeering clearly went on in London and the big cities, beyond it lay a good deal of less fundamentally criminal activity. As rationing began to bite, ordinary men and women, law-abiding in most respects, were tempted to cheat a little on the system to provide themselves with a little extra income or a few scarce luxuries. Country people, like the rest of the population, came to take a 'flexible' view of restrictions and were only too willing, when they had the chance, to try some petty profiteering. A black economy containing a strong element of bartering grew up alongside the official one based on ration books and cash.

Farmers were particularly well placed. Although any dealing in foodstuffs was illegal outside Ministry channels, the demand was guaranteed, and there were plenty of ways of meeting it. A cow might mysteriously injure itself and have to be slaughtered, the tally of sheep or pigs might be somewhat incomplete, or the foxes might be causing a terrible loss of poultry. On goods that were not actually rationed, there were other ways of making money: you could water the milk or overcharge for eggs and other items where the price was controlled. Heavy penalties awaited those who were caught, even if the offences were comparatively minor. Clive Hammersley of Hawthorne Farm at Ashley near Stoke-on-Trent was fined £20 for overcharging on eggs in July 1941. A witness in front of the stipendiary magistrate stated that she had bought eight small eggs from his market stall for 2s and later learnt from the Food Enforcement Officer that the price should have been 2s 6d per dozen. For selling milk containing added water, Edgar Clarke of South Littleton, Evesham,

Schoolboys at Burnt Yates, near Harrogate in Yorkshire, with scrap metal that they have collected from farms and fished out of streams.

was fined £30 by local magistrates in February 1944. An unnamed farmer who slaughtered '3 beasts and pigs without a licence or authority of the Ministry of Food' was sentenced to three months in prison, fined £100 and ordered to pay 25 guineas costs by Bury Justices in June 1942. The customers were also prosecuted: in Cornwall, the proprietor of the Truro Hotel was fined 100 guineas by St Austell magistrates for obtaining two slaughtered pigs illegally from the farmer, Harry Cobb of Manheirs, Creed, who was fined a total of £110 for supplying them.

There was evidence of bigger business in November 1944 when Robert Ware and his two sons were charged at Portsmouth with having run a slaughterhouse at a farm at Farlington Marshes in Hampshire. It was camouflaged as a rick of baled straw, with a tarpaulin roof and a concrete floor with a sump and slaughter equipment. The Wares were found out by Jack Lapham, a Special Constable, who heard, coming from what looked like a straw stack, men's voices and the sound of bones being sawn. Inside he found the carcases of a cow, two calves and three pigs. Roy Ware, one of the sons, made a statement taking full responsibility and claiming that he killed a cow that could not walk, and her two calves, and a pig that was lame. He was not believed, and all three men were commited for trial at Winchester Assizes.

Even giving food away could lead to a summons: Mrs Mary Upton, a poultry producer and Essex magistrate, was fined £10 5s at Chelmsford in February 1943 for having given butter and eggs from Coptfold Hall Farm to her relatives, friends and employees. However, this sort of prosecution was unusual, and the good sense of the local constabulary most often prevailed. The police seem to have turned a blind eye to a fair amount of 'helping out' between neighbours in the way of meat, dairy produce or fresh vegetables being exchanged for canned foods, coffee, spirits or perhaps some extra petrol. Any risk from the village bobby could be dealt with by his inclusion in what largesse was going. In one parish near Crediton in Devon, it was customary to put aside a shoulder of pork every so often to ensure official complaisance, while in the same county David St John Thomas recalls a similar ritual in South Molton:

I remember that we had some Devonshire cream delivered inside our front door, bang opposite the police station the very weekend after we arrived as evacuees. My father remonstrated with the dairy that Devonshire cream was on the taboo list for the war and what would happen if the police found out about it, and the dairyman said that trouble would be unlikely since, if my father liked to watch him, he would see him dropping a container at the police station before crossing the road to deliver it to us.

Poachers also managed to do nicely out of the war. Such traditional activities as the taking of rabbits and other game was not much worried about, as *Country Life* noted in January 1941:

In most villages there is at least one man who could always supply a rabbit. It may be impolitic to ask where it comes from, but in these days, when rabbits are a pest to the Ministry of Agriculture and a boon to the Ministry of Food, there is no need to be fussy. One-and-eight pence is the price the village trapper has been charging for a decent sized rabbit and if the skin is returned he pays 2d back. Someone comes round with a van each week and gives him 3d for the skins, and he tells me that he generally has five or six dozen to send away.

Inevitably, grazing animals presented a tempting target for more ambitious thieves, including hungry troops and unscrupulous townspeople. Sentencing a soldier to 18 months' imprisonment for stealing, Mr. Justice Croome Johnston said at Breconshire Assizes in February 1944 that in the circumstances the man had got off lightly since he could have imposed up to 14 years' penal servitude for the offence. Poaching was at its most organised for the Christmas trade, and poultry raids on the Cumberland-Scottish border in December 1944 were reported to be the most serious ever. As many as 20 geese or 50 poultry would disappear from some high-lying farms in a single night. Cyclists were blamed for many smaller thefts, but the big raids could only have been carried out by marauders in cars or lorries. 'At one time,' wrote *The Farmer & Stock-breeder*, reporting on the crime wave, 'the noise of night traffic might have awakened the inhabitants dogs on the farms, but the country districts are now accustomed, because of the war, to traffic at all times.'

In country districts, where the lines of supply could be very short, under-the-counter trade flourished. A greengrocer in Exeter prospered from innumerable small transactions with farmers' wives who brought him discreetly covered baskets of dairy produce, honey and other seasonal niceties every market day. Even small bunches of snowdrops and bags of field mushrooms were brought in to be sold at a respectable profit. David St John Thomas remembers a gentlemen's outfitters in South Molton where a bit of 'genteel jiggery-pokery' was carried on:

It was run by some sisters who looked very respectable, but if you wanted eggs they came out of the sock drawer and if you wanted butter they came out of the shirt drawer, and if you wanted this, that and the other thing it came out of various other drawers.

The risk, of course, was that shopkeeper and customer might be caught in the act by a visiting official. An efficient early warning system was soon established in the South Molton:

Every now and then you would suddenly be told to keep quiet or people would grimace at you. Once my mother was in a dairy when somebody came charging in and grimaced at the manager who disappeared into the back and despatched a few riders, who jumped on their bicycles and were all over the town in no time at all. Then you would have found the most regulated ration system, and anyone wanting anything off the ration would have been put very firmly in his place until the Inspector left from his visit a couple of days later.

Hoarding was another common wartime activity. In the early days of the war, when supplies were still to be had, prudent housewives saw nothing wrong in putting aside a few extra cans of this or that, small quantities of tea or sugar, or perhaps some tinned biscuits or block chocolate – just in case. When a German invasion seemed possible, a few went so far as to bury quantities of canned food in their gardens. Commenting that the chief trouble with this was remembering the location of the treasure trove, E.M. Delafield remarked 'the person who suggested marking it [the place] with a small tombstone in memory of an imaginary dog ought perhaps to have been taken more seriously at the time.' Later in the war, though, rationing was so tight there was nothing to hoard unless it was bought on the black market.

The Government's food programme was strictly enough policed that the black market was kept within bounds, and, relying for the most part on its official rations, the nation was better nourished in 1945 than it had been in 1939. Eating habits were changed with a skilful blend of control and cajolery – it was something of a joke among nutritionists that it had taken a national emergency to teach the British what to eat and how to cook.

Chapter 3
STRANGERS IN THE VILLAGE

War is coming 1941, they say. And there'll be plenty of broken crock-ery, and little houses ripped open like packing-cases, and the guts of the chartered accountant's clerk plastered all over the piano that he is buying on the never-never . . . It's all going to happen . . . There's no escape.

George Orwell's vision in his novel *Coming up for Air*, which was published in 1939, may have underestimated the proximity of the war, but it accurately reflected a growing sense of dread that was fuelled by the terrible example of German saturation bombing in the Spanish Civil War and by Winston Churchill's revelations of the frightening superiority of the Luftwaffe. It was expected that the declaration of war would immediately be followed by massive air raids on British cities resulting in the death of millions and bringing the country to a standstill. The government was not stirred into action until after the Munich crisis of 1938: it started to train ARP volunteers as firemen, wardens, ambulance drivers and nurses, to set up first-aid centres and issue gas masks to the civilian popu-lation. It also began to plan seriously for the evacuation of women and children. In January 1939, the Ministry of Health, which was in charge of the operation, undertook a national survey to see how many pregnant women, nursing mothers, children and invalids could be looked after in reception areas in the rural counties. Local auth-orities were asked to canvass householders to discover who would be willing to take evacuees. Some councils, like that of Lingfield in Surrey, responded keenly, setting up reception committees which made meticulous plans. Elsewhere, though, the response was often perfunctory and created difficulties when the war broke out and billeting became compulsory.

Some three million people were to be evacuated, the equivalent of twenty armies as large as the British Expeditionary Force and far less disciplined. After much initial confusion and scepticism about the feasibility of the whole operation, the plans were gradually worked out. By the late summer, Reception Committees everywhere had their instructions, and a number of practice evacuations had been successfully carried out. To cope with the shortfall of private accom-modation, a Camps Act was passed in Parliament to allow the setting up of fifty evacuation camps which in peacetime were to operate as holiday camps for 350 children each and would house considerably more in wartime. A generous budget of over a million pounds was provided but by November only six camps had been completed, as the building trade was in some disarray, with much of its workforce mobilised into the new war industries.

The pressure on accommodation was increased by the number of organisations that were to be evacuated. Country towns and seaside resorts were soon to contain rabbit warrens of civil servants, while such stately homes as were not taken over by the military were likely to be converted into maternity or convalescent hospitals. By the end of August, a number of organisations, including the BBC and some national newspapers, had finalised their plans for evacuation. So, too, had a number of public schools. All this was complicated by the fact that the emergency came at the height of the holiday season. As hotels emptied of people cutting short their holidays to return home, they were filled again by block-bookings. Farms and guesthouses also did an unexpected late trade – the faint-hearted flocked to the countryside, causing chaos at railway and coach stations as people recalled to their posts came up against the rush of others trying to get away.

On 1st September 1939, as Hitler's troops crossed into Poland, the evacuation began. Over the next three days, countless thousands of children were assembled in school groups, marched to railway stations and quickly put on waiting trains. A large part in the operation was taken by the W.V.S., which, with the Girl Guides and the Women's Institutes, had started to discuss evacuation plans as early as July 1938, two months before the Government started to take action. Within fourteen hours of the evacuation order, 120,000 women around the country were alerted by the W.V.S., and 17,000 worked as escorts in the initial stages. In the first three days of September 1939, one and a quarter million people were evacuated.

However, an operation that had been planned to work with military precision went somewhat awry. In their anxiety to get the children away, many dispatchers simply filled up trains as they came, with little attempt to keep to instructions. Schools were split up and often sent in quite the wrong direction. Muddle was made even worse by further improvisation en route and by the use of charabancs and private cars to complete journeys. Sometimes it took days or even weeks to track down 'the scattered', as they became known, by which time they had often been billeted with foster families.

The evacuation of London schoolchildren begins, 1st September 1939.

The frustration felt by the voluntary helpers at the reception areas was described by one of them, Frances Pitt, writing in *Country Life* on 23rd September 1939:

The tide of evacuation began to flow in our direction on the Friday before England declared war. 'Can you bring a car to the school at 5.30,' ran the message 'and take a few of the children to their billets?'

I went as instructed, but there were no children, only some twenty cars in waiting. The train was late. I returned an hour and a half later, to find about seventy little folk being refreshed in the school-room with cups of tea and bread and butter. Each one was carefully labelled and clung to a small bundle of belongings and the square box that enclosed the gas mask. Pathetic fingers clutched the boxes as if the masks were talismans that would steer them safely through this long and weary day to some haven, somewhere, some time or other. Two small boys and two girls sat on a school bench with tears running down their faces, but they wept quietly. For the most part the children were too tired and bewildered to cry. They just waited for something to happen. The majority made valiant efforts to drink their tea and eat their bread and butter, but what child could be expected to be lively at the climax of this hectic excursion? They were all tidy, well clothed, and looked as if they had come from good homes.

Twenty-four hours later came another call, this time for two cars to proceed to a local station and help distribute mothers and tiny tots. We found that some 500 of them had come and been taken to a nearby hall, where they were being given refreshments before being helped into a score of waiting buses and many private cars for con- veyance to their country distributing points. They were from the

Children from the East End of London, evacuated to Kings Langley in Hertfordshire on 2nd September 1939, eat their rations in Watford under the eye of Mr Farquharson (standing, second from left), Watford Corporation Manager, who has organised the reception arrangements.

The Thames paddle steamer *Crested Eagle* disgorges its load of East End evacuees at Felixstowe in Suffolk on 1st September 1939.

poorest quarters of the great city of Liverpool. Mothers with babies in arms and others hardly more than babies trailing at their heels stood about in groups. Some of these mothers were themselves little more than children, yet they looked old and experienced if not in years. The two young women I took away were of good class, most grateful for all that had been done for them and anxious to show their gratitude. All had to be got away, out into the countryside which to these dwellers in dark and narrow streets was a place of vast loneliness and fearsome terrors. Some of them, poor souls, were not, in health or hygiene, suited for such a translation, but anyhow they were not being bombed!

In his history of the W.V.S., *Women in Green*, published in 1948, Charles Graves recorded:

The fact that evacuation had happened during the school holidays had reduced the possibilities of medical inspection and cleansing beforehand. In the crowded trains, even children who were clean when they started their journey were infected with vermin and skin diseases by the time it ended. Nerve strain and fatigue, heat and hunger, the fear of the unknown perils they had escaped, and the unknown difficulties which lay ahead, made the evacuees less adaptable and ready to help themselves than they might otherwise have been. They also brought on enuresis among children not habitually dirty.

For children, the experience could be terrifying: after a long and tedious train journey, they arrived miles from home not knowing whether they would see their parents again, to be confronted by strangers who all too often haggled over which child they would take. The best dressed or most mannerly were likely to go first, leaving behind the children who were unattractive, sickly, bedraggled or too tearful. Evacuees from the slums were the most difficult to place, especially if they came from a large family of inseparable

Evacuated children discover the delights of blackberry picking in Buckinghamshire in September 1939.

brothers and sisters. The job of the billeting officer was a thankless one, as the pre-arranged schemes often had to be abandoned for a multitude of reasons. People who had expressed a preference for girls might get boys, while those who had been informed that they would be receiving expectant mothers found that they got mothers complete with families. Sometimes the mis-matches were extremely embarrassing, when vegetarian families found themselves billeted with carnivores or young orthodox Jews found themselves confronted every morning with rashers of breakfast bacon – a situation that was not unusual as there were many Jewish families among the evacuees from London's East End. A farmer's daughter from Haddenham in Cambridgeshire later recalled:

The evacuees sent to the village were mostly Jewish from the Whitechapel slum area. I shall never forget one of the first coachloads to arrive on a Saturday afternoon; there were a number of expectant mothers with young children. With their gas masks and bundles of belongings, they were a pathetic sight, frightened and bewildered and although they were given good homes and every care they could not settle! They missed the noise and bustle of Whitechapel with its fish and chip shops, its cinemas and pubs; before a week passed many returned home, preferring to be bombed out in London than to stagnate and die of boredom in a quiet country village.

Among the evacuees from the cities came refugees from Europe. One contributor to *The Farmers Weekly* in October 1939 noted that among the arrivals at Thetford in Norfolk was 'a German boy whose name was Adolf evacuated from Hackney. He had only been in England a fortnight. Also we had two Italian boys and a Polish boy who lived in the same house as the German boy. We called the German boy Fred.' Billeting continued to be a rather hit or miss affair, as *Country Life* remarked on 1st October:

84

Evacuation has now become rather like a game of poker. The local people make their discards, and every week the schoolmasters and evacuation officer shuffle the pack and make a fresh deal. By this means the apple-eating boy goes eventually to a fruitful Eden, the lady of confirmed ideas about the necessity for a pint of stout every evening finds other quarters than with the leading light of the temperance world, whose walls are covered with painted photographs of blue-ribboned, whiskered ancestors who held out on the teetotal front in the past.

The placing of evacuees was determined at worst by snobbery, by the wish to avoid 'problem' or 'ghetto' children of whom the hosts were likely to be ashamed, as well as by determination to minimise any intrusion on family privacy and settled ways. David St John Thomas remembers the arrival of one trainload of children at a North Devon railway station later in the war:

One night, a very long train, far longer than the length of the platform, arrived with literally hundreds of evacuees. All the cream of South Molton's society – the police and the magistrates and the town council – was at the station – to decide which families would receive which evacuees. Of course, that was a matter of considerable concern, because if you had somebody who looked as if their hair was infested with fleas or whatever, you wouldn't particularly want them in your house. Everything was determined at the station. It was like something out of Thomas Hardy, I suppose – a human cattle sale.

This contrasts with the picture painted at the time in *Illustrated* magazine of the scene at Lingfield, a small town with a population of under 5,000, where the cottage walls were said almost to bulge with happy evacuated children:

Lingfield recently billeted 200 children at a few hours' notice and without the slightest civic disruption. It was a great day for Lingfield. Private cars were in many cases waiting for them at the coach stop. Beaming, kindly faces awaited the guests.

Evacuees arrive at a Devon railway station.

Open-air schoolroom for evacuated London children, 9th September 1939.

85

In hundreds of cases there was no need for a wait in the dispersal centre. Most of the children were happily installed in their new homes, with a good meal awaiting them, within ten minutes of their arrival in the town . . .

Even after the evacuees had been found homes, there could still be sizable problems to be overcome. Many of the children from the slums were infested with lice, unused to soap and water and often ill-behaved. Sir William Beach Thomas voiced the shocked reaction of 'better-class' families who were accustomed to high standards of personal hygiene and spotlessly maintained homes:

It is as well for the sake of naked truth to acknowledge the real horror of the hosts towards both the ideals of their guests and their habits of body as well as of mind. Out of about 200 children received in one village exactly 40 had to be 'chemically cleaned', an ex-cottage hospital being converted for that purpose. One little girl, whose abundant but much neglected hair was altogether too populous, so

Left: children from Canning Town, Bow and Tottenham being read a bedtime story in December 1939 at the first home for evacuated under-fives, opened by Mrs Muriel Duncan at Knoll House, Uppingham in Rutland. Above: Mrs Holdsworth of Kingston Blount in Oxfordshire is helped by Joseph Hills, a farmer who is also the local Billeting Officer, to fill in the subsistence forms for her evacuees, two of whom look on.

At the opening meet of the Crawley and Horsham Foxhounds at Knapp Castle near Horsham in Sussex on 4th November 1939, the Hon. Mrs Walter Burrel snaps some evacuees who are staying in the district.

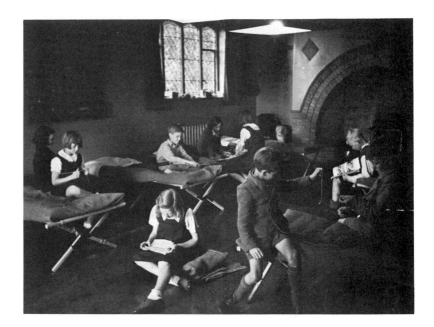

The billiard room of a large country house at Goring Heath in Berkshire becomes a dormitory for evacuees in the autumn of 1939.

enjoyed the hospital treatment that she begged to be allowed to go back there after the cleansing was complete. On the other hand, a small boy who was ordered by his hosts to take a bath, refused with oaths. He never did have a bath and did not see why he should.

A survey conducted by the National Federation of Women's Institutes among their members who had taken on evacuees produced a chorus of horror at the state of their charges. Some children from Liverpool had clothes that were stitched on and had to be cut off. The following reports dealt with evacuees from London, respectively from Vernon Square in King's Cross and from Bethnal Green:

The children were only accustomed to obey when cuffed or shouted at – this was true of at least 50 per cent. In quite a few cases the mothers had no control over their children at all and went home for that reason. One does not wish to be hard on these women, who of course were being seen at a disadvantage, but it is a fact that the poorest cottagers were shocked at their ignorance (of managing,

Evacuated children are taken for a walk in the grounds of the Duke of Connaught's mansion at Bagshot Park in Surrey, 25th September 1939.

cooking, etc.), at their lack of ordinary cleanliness and good habits.

Some were simply crawling with lice, etc., and actually *never* used a lavatory; the children simply sat down in the house anywhere to relieve themselves and actually one woman who was given the guest room . . . always sat the baby in the bed for this purpose.

Contact with houseproud country folk could also produce bewilderment – one lad writing home for the first time enclosed all his toffee-wrappings, apple cores and other scraps of rubbish because he did not know where to put them. Bed-wetting was a common problem in the early days, perhaps only to be expected afer the trauma of evacuation and adjustment to an alien lifestyle. It was working-class children who mainly suffered – being away from home was a novel experience for most of them, few having ventured further than a Sunday school outing or day trip to the seaside. Middle-class children, more used to holidays or to boarding school, soon recovered their self-confidence and could treat their new life as something of an adventure. For the lucky ones who were sent to stay with relatives in the country, there were family bonds to mitigate any feelings of homesickness.

There were, of course, exceptions. Some middle-class children were beset by shyness and hated country life, while young slum dwellers might have a natural cockiness and resilience that stood them in good stead. Some, indeed, were enchanted with the rural scene, as *The Farmers Weekly* noted a fortnight after the evacuation began:

The peaceful invasion of the countryside by the town youngsters may do far more than improve health. It may bring back an affection for the land which has been childless for too long. A few days ago I watched a very small person, complete with gas mask, in earnest conversation with a placid cow. They were infatuated with each other.

Frances Pitt also found:

. . . four children yesterday playing in the cottage garden, happy and contented, and such different children from what they were on the night of their arrival. Already there was new colour in their cheeks. They hugged the dog, they hugged the cat, they ran forth into the orchard to get apples (permitted ones), and then they dressed themselves up with greenery. The little girl made a skirt of marestails tied round her waist with a chain of fancy beads, and stood in smiling delight when I took her photograph. Then they were given baskets and sent off to get blackberries, which they did with cheery willingness. Everything was new to them, and all was lovely. For them the fields and hedges were a wonderland of joy.

It was the adult evacuees who were most likely to be impatient with country living. There were stories of evacuees asking where the village was and being told that they had just walked through it. Another evacuee, looking up the main street of the village, asked with a loud sniff where the pawn-shop was. When she was told that the village did not aspire to one, the sniff turned to a snort of contempt. 'No pawn-shop? Gawd! What a hole!' For the women who, in the eyes of their hosts, flocked hatless and stockingless into the countryside bent on a few days' holiday and were soon heartily sick of country people and their ways, the solution was simple: to go home without delay. The retreat started within a few days, and after a month – as no bombs fell – nearly half the mothers and a quarter of the children had returned to take their chances in their own neighbourhoods. They were tempted to go not just by what one woman

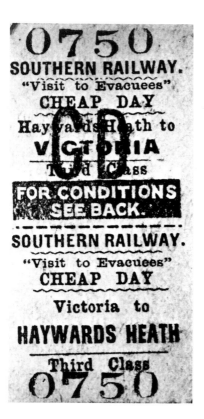

On a special 'Visit to Evacuees' cheap day return ticket, Mrs Carter goes to visit her children Michael and Angela in Sussex. She meets Mrs Cluton, with whom they are living, and says goodbye to them on Haywards Heath station.

called 'a purgatory of boredom' but also because they missed their jobs and good wages. Their return, although it caused misgivings, was not unwelcome, as the big cities had found themselves minus an army of packers, bottlers and factory workers just when they were most needed.

As Charles Graves noted in *Women in Green*, 'Not all the faults were on the side of the evacuees, for not all the billets offered to them were clean or desirable . . . there were some families with a low standard of living who considered that the billeting allowances would be a source of profit and were therefore anxious to pack in more unaccompanied children than they could properly accommodate.' Misconceptions about what awaited the evacuees did not help either:

Canvassers, anxious to induce as many mothers as possible to leave the target areas, had painted too rosy a picture of the accommodation which awaited them. Instead of the sunny cottage that would house the whole family . . . they found themselves in different billets from their elder children, and far from the shops and cinemas on which they had learned to depend.'

By the end of January 1940, 88 per cent of mothers had returned home, taking 86 per cent of children under school age with them. Even among Secondary School children, who settled best, only 57 per cent stayed evacuated. For those who went home, the return trips were not always uneventful. Confusion in designating 'evacuation' and 'neutral' zones led to some evacuated families being surprised on their return to discover their homes full of strangers: a woman who had been evacuated from Southampton arrived back to find that her house was occupied by an evacuated family from nearby Portsmouth. Much the same happened later in the war in Plymouth, which was amazingly classified as a neutral zone until 1941.

A few country people were overjoyed to be rid of their unwelcome guests. E.H. Baxter of South Sea Cove in the East Riding of Yorkshire wrote to *The Field* in February 1940 to say that he regarded evacuation as an 'experiment to please certain political and sociological cranks, to test certain subversive theories, and to harrass and annoy some of the best, finest and most stable elements in the realm, the country people.' He particularly abhorred government compulsion which forced them:

... to take into their homes adults and children whose standards of conduct and civilisation are far inferior to their own. This has not only meant serious financial losses, but the breaking up of family life and an enormous amount of work. The insanitary habits and destructive traits of the evacuees have increased the burden thrust on the householders. Their sacrifices are wholly unappreciated by townspeople and by the government, who have shown no sympathy with the unfortunate rural householders they have victimised. If air raids are coming many country people would prefer bombs to the evacuees they have got.

While most people would not have gone as far as Baxter in seeing the evacuation scheme as 'one of the worst and most cruel types of panic legislation', there were genuine and widely felt grievances, notably over the meagreness of the financial arrangements. For board and lodging a household received a basic 10s 6d for the first child and 8s 6d for each additional child. Clothing was to be provided by the parents – a problem with slum children who often possessed little more than rags. The better-off might simply buy new garments, but finding a change of clothes for the young could be a real worry for poor cottagers with large families. Expenditure on small personal necessities, extra fuel and lighting and wear and tear on the home were usually the subject of much wrangling with parents or local authorities. Nevertheless, only a few official adjustments were made. An additional laundry allowance of 3s 6d a week helped with the burden of chronic bed-wetters, and compensation was offered for infestation of bedding and for accidental or malicious damage to the homes of the hosts. The more sympathetic communities tried to help in sorting out the grievances, and organised sales of old clothes and recreational facilities for their guests. The Women's Institutes and W.V.S. also played their part in trying to integrate the newcomers and occupy their time by organising sewing bees, communal jam-making sessions and even discussion groups.

In February 1941, *The Farmers Weekly* ran a competition with a first prize of £15 for the best scheme to engage the energy and interest of the evacuees, adults as well as children, to the benefit of town and country alike. Letters poured in, many suggesting that the skills and training of townswomen could be used to remedy some of the deficiencies of rural life so that their country cousins could learn hairdressing, fashionable dress-making and secretarial work. Alternatively it was thought that the women evacuees might run a village laundry, communal feeding-centre or crèche. There was also the suggestion that a more useful step would be to let evacuee mothers take part in the domestic running of the household, even to the extent of sharing the kitchen. This was such a frequent source of friction that Mrs Arthur Webb, the Home Section editor of *The Farmers Weekly*, made a special appeal to her readers to 'let your evacuee guests join in the work. Nothing will so satisfactorily turn their minds away from the nightmare of tiredness and anxiety. Spare a little time to show them your ways and to show an interest in their methods too. Let them feel you want to learn some new ideas from them, and the odds are they will soon be proud of the new skills they are learning from you.' She continued encouragingly:

One farm I know, they were less than welcome when they arrived, but both households have settled down very happily through this exchange. The London boy and girl look after the two small farm children. The mother has taken over all the washing up and clearing away of meals, and is looking forward to tackling one of the twice-weekly bread baking as soon as she has got the hang of it.

Catering becomes a little easier if you remember that many things which are commonplace to you will be an excitement to town folk. Green vegetables, fresh from the garden, two kinds of them, with a generous dish of potatoes sprinkled liberally with parsley will be more interesting than meat to the woman who has had to queue for her greengroceries and has found very little choice at the end of the queueing. Your garden peas and beans – which she can gather and prepare for you – are to her a luxury. Onions and herbs made into good forcemeats and served with a very little meat, cheese or bacon will very likely be a novelty. You have much more chance than the townswoman of making really deliciously flavoured gravies; and your home-made chutneys and relishes need ingredients that just haven't been in city shops.

On the other hand, urban catering has inevitably meant more tinned food and a long habit has made many townpeople prefer it. Plenty of them, offered fresh salmon, would dislike the flavour and prefer the canned variety . . . a crisis unlikely to occur these days, but symptomatic. Tinned pilchards, herrings or salmon flaked into macaroni and mixed with a cheese sauce is an easy economical dish which you could ask your guests to prepare for you while you were busy elsewhere. If you haven't macaroni, try the same mixture with sliced cooked potatoes.

Boiling bacon, which the country home can sometimes supply, may have to be an acquired taste for those less familiar with it. But I never knew a town family yet that didn't look on Yorkshire pudding as a treat; and adapted either with herbs as a savoury, or with a really lavish filling of sausagemeat or mince (or again canned fish) as toad-in-the-hole, or with a scatter of dried fruit as a sweet to be eaten with syrup or jam, you can also give them something here that will be a luxury.

Your guest may herself have valuable ideas to contribute about various ways of serving tinned chopped ham or luncheon pork. If not, try chopping it small, heating it with a little fat in a pan, and stirring it into rice that you have fried and then simmered in stock.

A young evacuee, still wearing her luggage label, begins to relax by the sea.

91

Get her, again, to do this for you; ask her to help in such ways that she will feel herself a part of the household.

Some country people went further than Mrs. Webb's rather patronising compromise and felt that they had a duty to educate their town guests in culinary matters, if only because of the appalling eating habits of many slum children. Breakfasts of porridge or bacon and eggs were sometimes greeted with consternation by cockney urchins who claimed that they breakfasted at home on bananas and beer or chips and ale. But fresh food and home cooking were soon to work wonders with undernourished city children, most of whom put on weight and gained in health and vitality. Indeed, the temptations of overindulgence offered by plentiful country food sometimes meant recourse to the castor oil.

While the boys took enthusiastically to the joys of scrumping fruit, the girls might find themselves initiated into the mysteries of home economics. They might be expected to help with the jam or chutney making or to prepare home-reared meat for the table. Those of a sensitive disposition, accustomed to buying food in shops, were likely to be distressed by their first sight of a chicken's neck being wrung. One girl on a South Devon farm 'cried a good deal' when she came to remove the innards and feathers and found sausage-making equally distasteful. In remote districts, the living conditions could be disconcerting: cottages could be dark, dank and badly overcrowded – without electricity or running water, services that were taken for granted even in the poorer inner city areas. In the blackout, having to go to an outside privy that was usually an earth closet at the bottom of the garden could be an unnerving experience. For the more robust, like Lily, who was sent from London to Mundford in Norfolk, the difference between domestic arrangements in town and country could be fascinating:

I asked the lady where the tap was, and she said 'It is standing on the stool.' I was rather taken aback when she said that, but I soon found out the water was in two buckets. The water is pumped or drawn from a well and they keep it in buckets.

Some of the people here have electric light because they make their own, but we use oil lamps. I have learnt how to look after an oil lamp. Our food cupboard, as we call it in London, is a room, and it did feel strange walking into a food cupboard.

A precocious teenager was more preoccupied by social differences:

I used to live in London, but now live in the country and I like it very much. Country people are quite different and seem to know an awful lot about what they do know and not much about anything else.

They don't know much about wild flowers, and just call them all weeds. They say things that make me want to hoot they are so silly, but they are pretty quick, and if you laugh at them you can be sure they'll be laughing at you the next minute.

They don't like to believe anything in books, but sometimes do if they agree with it.

I thought things like class distinctions had faded out long ago, with the introduction of buses and better education; but here they certainly haven't. Maybe it is because there aren't many buses and education is treated with contempt.

Anyway there are two main sorts of people here – the toffs, as they call them, and the ordinary folk. Ordinary folk are the working class upwards and the toffs are the ones with money. Any attempt on the part of a member of either class to become too friendly with the other class is looked on with suspicion.

About 120,000 schoolchildren were evacuated from Greater London in June 1940, mainly to the West Country and Wales. Here a crowd of them are on their way to the station.

The equality of man doesn't exist for country people, because on every hand they have proof that man is not equal. In London people seem more equal because when a lot of different people are on a bus the conductor can turn any of them off the bus whether it's Lady Thingumebob or a navvy, and really the conductor is the ruler of the bus and the people on it. But in the country Lady Thingumebob would probably own the conductor's house and it is she who is the ruler. And, anyway, he would never have the opportunity of turning her off the bus, because she would never be on it, though that is beginning to happen a bit now.

Sometimes I long for the nice middle-class feel of a London bus. Then there is this courting business. I giggled when they asked me if I was courting, but it turned out that they meant it, and I didn't know what to say. Their idea is that if you so much as go to a dance with a boy you will marry him in the end. It makes things very difficult and I expect I've got a pretty poisonous name round here by now. Of course, they all know your business and often tell you where you were the evening before and who with and tell you not to take so long saying good-night next time. This all sounds as if I hate the country. Actually I don't, and everyone is really very nice – to your face. There I go again . . . But they do gossip and pull you to pieces and start dreadful rumours. Still, that's what I really like best about the country – there is always so much to talk about.

Most of the evacuees who remained in the countryside over the winter and into the spring of 1940 settled in and found life was much more tolerable than they first expected. The fall of France in May and June initiated a second wave of evacuees, this time from the coastal areas of Suffolk, Essex, Kent, Sussex and Hampshire. The fear of invasion drove those closest to peril to seek safety further west or north. More than a third of a million people were moved away from the coast during the summer, leaving such towns as Brighton, Bognor Regis, Yarmouth, Margate and Felixstowe virtually deserted except for military personnel. The government was anxious to get the inhabitants of the town away as quickly as possible, but advised people in the countryside generally to stay put, fearing that panic-stricken refugees would jam the roads and prevent troops getting to the front.

The new exodus, swollen by the Blitz, which started with the all-night raid on London on 23rd August 1940, put accommodation under extra pressure, and not everyone responded as generously or patriotically as might have been hoped. *The Field* commented in its 9th November issue that, unlike the humbler countryfolk, many better-off families were failing in their duty to take in evacuees from the battle zone:

Take just one rural area – one we know well – as an example. Almost every small house and almost every labourer's cottage has its quota, sometimes more than its quota, of evacuees. The hosts and hostesses have, almost without exception, accepted them willingly and have done their utmost, often on pitifully inadequate incomes and at great personal inconvenience, to make them feel happy and at home. And the evacuees, many of them with bitter experiences behind them, not a few with no worldly possessions at all, the victims of senseless brutal murder from the skies, have done their best to fit in and to help. Some will never return to London if they can help it, for they have in the country found a peace and a quietude that before they did not know existed.

But there is another side to the picture in this particular rural area. Here there are a number of large houses, and a considerably larger number of fairly large houses. Very few have any evacuees, and of those that have, very few make any real attempt to do anything for their guests. The evacuee is regarded as an unmitigated nuisance, as a creature from another world. And it is true of course: they are creatures from another world – the world of the bombed. But it is foolish, and an un-English attitude, and one that deserves the strongest condemnation.

Not all the evacuees in May and June 1940 were human. Livestock were evacuated from vulnerable areas around the south and east coasts. Here some of more than 100,000 sheep from Romney Marsh that went as far afield as Somerset and Warwickshire are being loaded on a special train.

There are exceptions, happily. We hear of a lady who has bought a large country house, and turned it over to sixteen families bombed out of their homes. And she pays all expenses. We know of a gentleman with a country mansion, who has moved into a small house in his grounds, and turned the mansion over to the authorities for the use of evacuated persons of advanced age and small income who have been bombed out, or who are too infirm to remain in danger areas. We cannot all do that sort of thing. But we can all do something.

England, to-day, may be divided into two classes – the bombed and the unbombed. The bombed have had their share. It is up to the unbombed, and not only the unbombed of limited means and limited accommodation, to help those less fortunate . . . There are 270,000 more children to be taken out of London, and many more adults. And there are any number of spare bedrooms among the great unbombed.

The alternative to private billeting was communal housing whether in hostels, in accommodation under local authority control or in evacuation camps. One of the most successful communal schemes was organised by Kingsbridge Rural District Council in Devon and was described in *Illustrated* by Stephen Black in April 1942:

I have just visited a rural area in England where 14,000 live under a 'Soviet system.'

But no one calls it by that name.

The people of this rural 'Soviet' are the women and children evacuees from blitzed cities and danger areas. They live communally, their lives being ordered much like those of the Russian peasants in the best collective farms of the Soviet Union.

A dormitory in a communal billet for evacuees.

They work together, look after their children together, and have their amusements together.

Cots in the infants' dormitory in a communal billet.

There probably, the comparison ends, for whatever complaints are made – and could 14,000 people be torn from their homes without complaints? – are usually connected with the fact that the people themselves have no representative on the 'Soviet'.

Let's look at the system in operation as evacuation nears the end of its third year. It is to be found in the rural district of Kingsbridge, Devon, which, by British political standards, is and always has been true-blue Tory.

These evacuees are among the happiest in the country.

Before the war began, Kingsbridge Rural District Council set up a Civil Defence Committee with the declared object of 'dealing with everything arising out of the war.' But as soon as the war started the Committee soon found that evacuees' problems took up more than eighty per cent of its time at the bi-weekly meetings in the Rural Council Chamber.

So it got down to the organisation of communal billeting all over the 110 square miles of countryside well known to peace time holiday-makers.

A cabinet of directors was formed: a director of housing; a director of activities; a director of supplies; a director of health; even a director of gardens.

The Committee acting on the authority of the Ministry of Health

Children sleeping in a communal billet, and a mother and child from New Cross in London enjoying the sunshine of South Devon, where they are staying in a Ministry of Health communal billet.

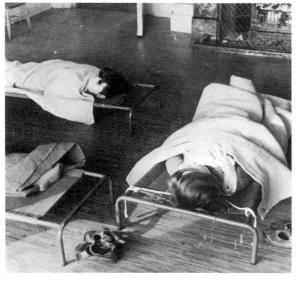

As the sun goes down, 40 children from Blackfriars and Gravesend who are billeted at Dartington Hall at Totnes in Devon return from a walk with their teacher.

requisitioned 160 country houses, bungalows, country cottages and villas with a total rental value of £10,000 per annum.

The director of gardens got down to work to raise fresh fruit and vegetables from the land that went with the houses.

When evacuees began to stream into Kingsbridge, they were shown at once into well-organised, clean and homely communal billets. Beds, blankets, cleaning materials and all the essentials of communal furniture were available.

The director of health instituted a health insurance scheme on a 3d per week contribution. Even visiting husbands from the forces, from London, Bristol, Plymouth were catered for in week-end cottages known as 'The Love Nest' and 'Honeymoon House'. Here the mothers could join their husbands for holidays away from the communal life of the big houses.

The director of activities organised some activity for nearly every night of the week – adult education, sewing classes, film shows, whist drives, dancing and community singing.

Under the Kingsbridge scheme mothers living in community billets pay 14s 6d weekly, 6s 6d for each child over 5, and 4s 6d for each child under 5.

Those who work in the kitchens get paid for it. Each mother makes her own bed and helps to clean her room. There is a hot dinner every day with meat, two veg. and 'afters.' There is high tea, and a good breakfast.

The mothers work in the gardens if they wish. So do the children. The director of gardens is himself a market gardener. Even if the schools are overcrowded, the kiddies are still happy and spend much time out of doors. They collect salvage, go fruit picking for jam making, climb trees, walk in the fields and wood.

Even Chessington Zoo is evacuated to South Devon and bus loads of evacuees visit it frequently.

At Dartington Hall, Totnes, 150 Blackfriars and Gravesend children are housed communally in the Junior School building. A salaried

London boys from the Rotherhithe Nautical School in Bermondsey exercise on the sands at Ferryside in Carmarthenshire.

house father organises their out-of-school activity. They have boating on the river, boxing in the winter. Normal education continues amidst ideal surroundings under L.C.C. teachers.

Each communal community has its social centre; each communal billet its recreation room, child welfare clinic, nursery school with qualified Froebel teachers.

The evacuees of Kingsbridge are among a great army scattered throughout the country, which still numbers 800,000 despite the large numbers who have gone home.

They cost the country £15,000,000 a year – the bill for one day of war. Is the money well spent?

Since it lets a new generation grow up in healthy surroundings, the answer should be yes.

There were still some evacuees who had to find their own future. *Farmer & Stock-breeder* found one particularly resourceful mother:

Coming from a badly blitzed area with twin boys aged 15, the little seamstress had been offered temporary refuge in a garage which

Two classes from Woodmansterne Road School, Streatham, London, in the village hall at Farmers, Carmarthenshire.

Boys from Stanley Street School, Deptford, London, take a morning dip in a Pembrokeshire lake.

had once housed expensive cars. It had a stove, and hot-water pipes running the length of one wall.

The boys immediately obtained work on a nearby farm, while the mother helped for 4 hours daily in the dairy. Between the whiles she endeavoured to make a home from home until hostilities ceased and her husband returned from the Far East.

At one end of the garage was a lobby with a window but no door. A number of thin bags given by the farmer were unpicked, washed and dyed dark blue. From these and laths of old Venetian blinds the evacuee constructed a door for her own private apartment and screens for her sons' 'bedroom'. The blitz-scarred beds and pillows she had managed to salvage were given an outer casing of white drill made from the better parts of discarded milking overalls. Much exquisite mending was camouflaged by floral designs on pillow-cases.

The large windows of the garage were fitted with outside shutters. Inside, gracefully draped net curtains appeared to have had a handful of flower petals thrown onto them. Examination showed that artificial petals and leaves had been appliquéd to conceal rents caused by splintered glass. A daintily frilled pelmet covered the peeled hazel rods.

Pegged rugs of navy and red cloth relieved the bareness of the concrete floor and added a colourful note to this 'make-do' home.

The luckiest children were, not surprisingly, the pupils of famous public schools that were wholly relocated in a country mansion or hotel where board and lodging were supplied. Westminster boys went to Lancing in Sussex, St. Paul's boys to Lord Downshire's estate near Wokingham, while those from Malvern College found themselves living in considerable grandeur at Blenheim Palace. Public school girls did equally well: Rodean was evacuated to the Keswick Hotel in Cumberland, while Benenden re-assembled at a hotel at Newquay in Cornwall. Some other secondary schools were

Plymouth children being taken to the railway station to be evacuated in July 1941.

also fortunate: Sheffield High School was sent to Calver in the heart of Derbyshire and Queen Ethelburga's School, Harrogate, removed to Studley Royal near Ripon in Yorkshire an estate with the ruins of Fountains Abbey in its park. A number of London primary school children were lodged at Laycock Abbey in Wiltshire, where, a century earlier, William Henry Fox Talbot had done his early photographic experiments; there were lessons in the South Gallery and the Crypt was used as a cloakroom.

The headmistress of a girls' public school noted the changes in curriculum and the pitfalls of teaching in the country:

We have done more practical and less book work here . . . The war has meant first-aid lectures and demonstrations, cookery for the older girls in case their services might be needed, the growing of vegetables, making clothes for evacuees in the neighbouring villages, and, of course, much knitting. But we have not allowed the academic work to suffer. I think, indeed, the older girls have worked with less effort – perhaps due to the lovely air and the sense of security. . .

How to give this atmosphere of safety and the peaceful life so necessary for young girls without ignoring the war is a real problem for those in charge of youth. Remote from bombs, 'planes and gun-fire, as many of the schools so far have been – and, let us hope will continue to be – it is almost possible for them to *forget* the war, yet they must not do so. They should not be scared or alarmed, or learn too much of the horrors of modern warfare, but wise head-mistresses know that their elder girls must not be shielded from the knowledge of contemporary life, of which war, alas! is now a part.

Even in remote districts there is the wireless, and newspapers arrive – it may be, many hours late – and discussions take place on current events, and the girls are encouraged to work, save, and spend for the Services in which many of their fathers and brothers are fighting.

With younger children, the priority was to distract them from homesickness and fear of the blitz. Miss Kathleen Monypenny diverted her infants by taking them on nature walks:

We generally take the bigger threes, fours and fives for walks twice a day in this lovely part of Buckinghamshire: at first they were oblivious to everything but the sound of an oncoming car or an aeroplane.

Now after four months, minds and eyes have become used to the new surroundings and the new ways, the routine is familiar as discoveries are being made every day. Snow, for instance, is not only wet: it is hard and white. No animal likes being shouted at, it moves away. A hedge is not a lot of dead sticks: and you must not pull off bits.

When I told them they would never hear the wind nor the cows and horses munching grass, nor see a rabbit, if they made such a noise, I thought it had made no impression at all. The only sound they could detect was a 'mo'or car' or lorry. But two days later Raymond, an apparently unimaginative little boy, stood stock still and said softly: 'Listen, the wind.'

The impression was instantaneous. Everyone's voice was suddenly stilled. The children stood where they were to hear the little wind among the autumn branches, and for a breathless second we seemed indeed not far from Heaven. Long after, when a late bird whistled loudly in a tree above our heads, and they heard it, I was as thrilled as were the children.

Some schools were more ambitious, setting out to enlist pupils' interest in their own small farm. At Odam Hill School in North Devon, care was taken to introduce the youngest and most timid pupils to kittens and sheep dog puppies first, so that these more familiar animals would form a link between 'home pets and strange new creatures, such as ducks, chickens and goats'. For those a year or two older, there were more responsible tasks to be undertaken:

The herd of goats is the chief feature of the farm, and there is a model goat stable in which the milking nannies are housed. Each stall is labeled with the name of the goat occupying it, and a row of

Plymouth children, evacuated after the first air raids on the city, in the very different surroundings of a West Country village.

buckets in the dairy and a grooming brush for each goat, bearing the owner's name hangs in its appropriate place.

The children take a very active part in the management of goats, and under the supervision of a grown-up person they do the milking, grooming, feeding and cleaning out the stables. The milk is carefully recorded in a milk book and simple accounts are kept to show the profit and loss on the herd, and at the same time the children learn elementary book-keeping without realizing it!

Lingfield Central School also had its own farm, with an impressive list of activities:

Every morning and afternoon evacuated children can be seen at work . . . They have a pen of pigs to feed and care for, an apiary for studying the life of the bee, and each child has his own fork, spade and hoe.

They are growing experimental wheat and clover. They collect acorns to feed the pigs and have grown fodder to feed the chickens and pigs in winter. They have built a body on to their field tractor, erected a fine tool shed, cemented the floor of the pig sty, made an ornamental pool and garden, and they grow most of the vegetables for the canteen (60 lb of cabbage a day).

Not all rural education was so successful – some mothers deplored the lack of facilities and the overcrowding when one village school had to serve several villages and hamlets as well as the evacuees. The long trudge to school in every kind of weather might be far from beneficial to the health, as Mrs Dodd, evacuated to Shropshire with her daughter insisted in *The Farmers Weekly* in August 1941:

I have lived here since August 30th, 1939. If this village is typical I feel that many reforms were needed long before evacuation was heard of. The village children have for generations left home at 6 a.m., always in Wellington boots (unsuitable for all-day wear however admirable for other purposes), for their 2½-mile trek over the fields (their midday meal a packet of sandwiches at best) and come home at 4 p.m., weary, past-hungry, often soaked. The 1939 evacuees, my own six-year old included, did the same. I was told:

'The country walk will work wonders.' It did. She was soon as sickly as the rest, coming home thoroughly knocked-up and dispirited, too far gone to tackle a good meal.

Country people, for their part, were not altogether sure of the value of nature study expeditions for town-bred children. One contributor of a sporting bent wrote to *Country Life* in December 1939 that letting them follow the hunt might be more beneficial:

Sir, – One of the few good things which have so far come out of this war is, it seems to me, the way in which our children evacuees are taking to country ways. *Per contra* the most unpopular of their lessons is now the 'Nature Walk,' where their master instructs them in the book knowledge of birds and flowers. They drag their feet, slouch miserably, look as cold as Hottentots on an ice flow and hate nature with all the concentrated venom of afflicted youth. It is impossible not to sympathise with them, and the worthy lady of the village who said that the urban teachers should 'learn to look for the nits before looking for birds nests in November!' condenses local opinion. But when hounds meet, what a difference! A hundred and twenty London school children (without any teacher, as it is Saturday) give tongue as hounds move off. It is strange music and the face of the Master colours; the grim huntsman is a philosopher, but it is a trying moment. The children reach the covert a little before the puzzled hounds and vanish into it with Bedlam noises. Three hours later they drag back

14-year-old Teddy Neale from Shepherds Bush in London brings back the afternoon's catch of rabbits in August 1944 on a Cotswold farm at Stanton, near Broadway, where he is billeted with his mother and sister. His father is a London Transport bus driver on the 28 route.

Boys from Westminster School, evacuated to Herefordshire, working on the land in their spare time in January 1941.

from points four or five miles away, thoroughly tired, covered with mud, and gloriously happy. They add their quotas to the difficulties of war-time hunting, but it is one of the most genuine demonstrations of a real love of sport. Good luck to the little horrors, for hunting is one of the few subjects their tiresome pedagogues have not lectured them upon. It still remains a sport – HBCP.

More serious observers deplored the failure of the educational system to teach children the basics of agriculture. The example of the best few schools and their school teachers could not make up for years of neglect, the net result of which created an almost unbridgeable gulf between town and country. The practical costs of urban children's ignorance could be serious, with innumerable instances of damage to crops by urban trespassers. Farmers and rural authorities could on occasion react in a needlessly oppressive way. Thus the suggestion that a competition for catching cabbage white butterflies should be organised among schoolchildren was turned down by Newton Abbot Urban District Council in Devon in July 1941 on the grounds that evacuees billeted in the district could not be trusted to do the job.

Some rural authorities were reluctant to accept evacuees at all, or at least no more than the minimum quota of them, alleging that they disrupted agricultural work, particularly in areas where farmers depended on part-time female labour for the planting, hoeing and harvesting of market garden and horticultural crops. Staplehurst in Kent and Wisbech in Cambridgeshire protested during the course of 1940 that women would be unable to perform their usual seasonal farm tasks if required to care for children, a plea that was in both cases overruled by the Ministry of Health. Individual farmers also tried to challenge the government with a similar lack of success. A Devon farmer, Frederick Marshall of Lower Mead Farm at Ashburton, was fined £5 with 2 guineas costs in August 1944 for failing to comply with the billeting order to take in two 13-year-old boys from a flying bomb area. Marshall argued that apart from not being in a very good state of health, he was too busy to take in children and would take his chance with the law courts. They, however, clearly agreed with the prosecuting officer that 'Marshall was setting a shocking example, one that others might follow, causing the position to become chaotic.'

Yet evacuee children with the right encouragement and instruction could prove themselves adept at some farming tasks. Quick young hands were ideal for setting potatoes or weeding, or for gleaning corn after it had been harvested. There were openings for those with entrepreneurial talents: a party of about fifty boys and girls, chiefly from Hull, assisted on farms in the Epworth area on a contract basis, which brought them a well-earned reward for after-school activity. Some of the young evacuees who worked in the volunteer labour camps enjoyed the experience so much that they sought a career in farming after the war. Special training schemes were set up to encourage what was seen as the nucleus of a back-to-the-land movement, and one in Devon succeeded to the extent that evacuee boys outnumbered those from the county itself. At a meeting in January 1941, one farmer urged the local War Ag to do something to interest Devon parents in placing their sons on the land – 'otherwise we shall all be learning Cockney rhyming slang in the future'.

Other schemes were put in hand to help refugees reconstruct their future in agriculture. The most notable was run by the International Commission for War Refugees near Market Rasen in Lincolnshire. A manor house was modernised to accommodate teenagers from France, Belgium, Germany, Hungary and the Channel Islands. The land was used to teach boys the most up-to-date methods of scientific farming, while the girls specialised in domestic economy. American foster-parents paid for the children's keep and allowed them pocket money. After they had been trained, the Ministry of Labour provided each with an Alien's Work Permit, which allowed them to be placed on farms.

Apart from its semi-permanent new population of evacuees, the countryside also acted as host to people taking a few days' respite from war work or fighting. In addition to pre-war holiday accommodation, country houses also provided popular rest places for frontline workers such as firemen, first aid workers, air raid wardens, members of rescue demolition squads and people employed in key industries in London and the large provincial cities. Some properties were offered voluntarily – a man living in a 'safe area' in the South Midlands offered a weekend's break 'in his own home at his own expense, for any two couples or party of four friends, who are in need of it and can arrange to get away from Friday until Tuesday morning.' He used to give them 'a thoroughly restful time' and 'a sitting room to themselves' if they wanted it. All they had to do was to pay their own train fares.

Other properties were officially requisitioned, some as 'country

Left: even before the outbreak of war, a group of fifty Jewish boys and girls, refugees from Germany and Austria, were being taught farming at Tingrith Manor Farm in Bedfordshire. Here, in May 1939, some of the boys are learning to handle a plough. Below: girl refugees from the Channel Islands at Marple in Cheshire trying on new shoes and clothes presented by American sympathisers.

Two young evacuees from Islington in London help on a farm at Porthcurno in Cornwall in April 1941.

clubs' for the services. Sailors had the use of a Hampshire mansion which included a nine-hole golf course, lawn tennis court, a cricket pitch and a croquet lawn. Indoors were billiards, table tennis and a well-stocked bar. The 4s 6d a day that it cost petty officers and ratings to stay for the weekend was considered a bargain.

Not all rest homes were so luxurious, and some, especially those for the blitzed, were merely improvised shelter organised by voluntary relief agencies. Hinneger Camp, on the Duchess of Beaufort's estate, consisted of 31 camouflaged tents, each of which could take five mothers in camp beds with cradles and cots for the children. Every Friday during 1941, 45 bombed-out mothers and children left Bristol Rest Centre for a fortnight's holiday at the camp, which was run by the Lord Mayor's Air Raid Distress Fund. The holiday-makers were greeted by the Camp Commandant Hilda Pole and her assistant, Monica Walter. They were then, disconcertingly, issued with waterproofs and gum boots; ration books were handed over, and the whereabouts of wash-houses, dining room and kitchens established. With that, the holiday could begin and wartime worries could be, if not actually forgotten, at least kept at a distance.

Many Land Girls, however, wanted to escape from the countryside into the city for their relaxation. They were catered for in the W.L.A. Rest House in London. Opened in June 1941, No. 2 Chesham Street offered Land Girls a place to stay in the capital 'where they could bring their friends to meals and be sure of giving them better hospitality, in more pleasant surroundings, than they could find in most hotels. The place could sleep 20 girls at a time and serve up to 100 at a meal. The Minister of Agriculture's wife designed the canteen decorations, which were described in *The Farmers Weekly* as 'gay and charming', while upstairs each bed had either a patchwork quilt sent from the United States or a knitted coverlet from Canada. The charges were 3s a night or 15s a week for bed, bath and breakfast. A two-course meal (beef, vegetables and pudding) with coffee cost 1s 2d. Scarcely had the hostel opened, though, than the doodle bug menace once more brought death from the skies and yet another evacuation of the cities.

The air raids on London reached another peak in February 1944, and in June, with the arrival of the first flying bombs, a quarter of a million women and children were officially evacuated from the city,

Soldiers manning an anti-aircraft battery occupy their spare time by growing their own vegetables.

some for the second or third time, while perhaps half a million more sought temporary respite in the countryside on their own initiative. As before, some of them had only just left the capital when others decided that their action had been too hasty and started back again. Mr. Churchill raised a laugh in the House of Commons in August when he commented that many of the trains, including some of the relief trains, had returned nearly as full as they went out. Nevertheless, many evacuees stayed in the countryside for nearly the whole course of the war, often establishing friendly relationships that lasted into peacetime.

Other wartime strangers in the village were the thousands of British and American troops stationed in the countryside. In the main, they were warmly received, although a farmer's daughter from Haddenham in Cambridgeshire noted the startled reaction of local gipsies to the arrival of searchlights:

Several army units were stationed in the village during the war and many of the men were billeted with local families. A Yorkshire regiment, the R.A.M.C. and an American searchlight party stayed quite a while . . . Searchlights were used a great deal during the war, moving across the sky to search for enemy planes. I remember when they were first used, my father went down to the Fen early one morning to find a number of frightened and excited gipsies on The Cut bridge, who could not understand what was happening to the heavens. They knew all about the moon and the stars but these frightening, glaring lights flashing about the sky caused them much alarm and kept them awake all night. It took my father some time to explain to them and calm their fears.

Many of the soldiers missed the familiar amusements of town life just as keenly as the evacuees. A.E. Bullivant wrote in *Country Life* in December 1940 of the village where he was billeted:

Here there are no cinemas nearer than, perhaps, seven miles, no League football, no greyhound tracks, no palatial dance-halls, no bright cafes, no lively public houses, no late editions. All the complexities that make up ordinary town life are missing, and for a time, the loss seems irreparable.

Sooner or later, local interests and hospitality went much of the way towards filling the gap, and soldier visitors were accepted 'with that camaraderie which uniform often seems to introduce. We are admitted at once to confidences which the ordinary stranger rarely obtains. For us there is no suspicion, no "standoffishness".' The kindness of country people did much to alleviate feelings of homesickness among the Commonwealth troops. A Canadian officer from Winnipeg recalled how he appreciated spending Christmas leave among ordinary family life in a farm house:

I've been one of the lucky ones, I had a fine Christmas. The people acted like I was real welcome you know, made you feel a real chap again, talking about ordinary things. Not all the other fellers was lucky. They're good to you at the Soldiers' Club, too; but what you get to want real bad is ordinary folks to talk to about ordinary things. You know, somewhere you can be yourself and forget all the rest of the army for a bit.

The arrival of the Americans was the most momentous event of the war in many rural areas, not least because they came in such overwhelming numbers. It was the first time that many countrymen, like David Shirra of Longden near Shrewsbury, had seen a non-white. 'A convoy of Americans stopped on the main road, some were black. I had never met a black man before and they gave us gum, sugar and biscuits.' In one village where the population was increased tenfold by the arrival of the Americans, one very old villager was not surprised to be visited by black soldiers, but remarked, 'I like them Americans. But who be the white chaps they'm brought along with them?'

Surprisingly, there seems to have been little colour prejudice on the part of country people. Indeed, as David St John Thomas recalls, the locals might even side with the blacks:

One night there was a major riot in South Molton. It was caused by a fight between black and white Americans in which, to the utter astonishment of American whites, the whole town took the side of the blacks. The reason for the quarrel was one that South Molton people would be very appreciative of – they like any debt being honoured to the last penny. A black soldier had got a loan off a local

Hampshire Down and Oxford Down sheep tended by the airmen of RAF Aston Down in Gloucestershire graze around a Spitfire.

person just before South Molton became white American territory and was put out of bounds to the American blacks, and this guy wanted to repay the loan. He was refused permission to come into the town, but eventually he slipped through in the back of a local car and was seen near the police station by an American white who assaulted him for disobedience. Well, the fact that a white hit a black was enough for the South Molton people, but the fact that he hit him when the black man was there repaying a debt was just too much and the entire population rose in arms against the white American troops.

American soldiers accept the hospitality of the regulars at a pub at Slapton in Devon, the day before the pub is closed and the village begins to be evacuated so that the area can be used in rehearsals for the D-Day landings. The rehearsals ended in disaster when German E-boats caught the unprotected landing craft unawares at Slapton Sands and 749 GIs were killed.

Cyril Maddox from Whixall in Shropshire also remembers colour being the cause of fights between GIs:

We met the Yanks at the dances, and got on well with them. There was hardly any friction between them and the local youths, but between the black and white Yanks it was a different story. Eventually it was blacks out one night and whites out the next. I always thought the blacks were quieter. They would do a turn – singing or playing the piano – at Wem Town Hall. That was very enjoyable.

The presence of troops at a local 'do' meant keen competition for the village lads. The Americans, in particular, were resented for their smart appearance, with uniforms of a superior cut and quality, for their money and endless supply of small luxuries. In his Home Guard battledress Cyril Maddox felt at a considerable disadvantage:

At the local parish-room dance there would always be lots of R.A.F. men, some Americans, the odd Canadian, Australian or New Zealander and later there were some Dutch and Polish chaps – all in uniform and with more money than we had. You can imagine we local lads had a very thin time of it.

Not all the country girls were swept off their feet by the sudden abundance of eligible young men. It was flattering, of course, to be wooed by an American with candies, stockings and perfume – unobtainable luxuries under rationing – and exciting to meet a man whose home was thousands of miles away on another continent and who talked in the accent of movie stars. It might also be enticing to be offered a lift in a jeep at a time when travel was so restricted. But while many girls fell for the easy charm and go-getting approach of the GIs, others were put off by their familiarity and brashness. Loyalty to a boyfriend in the forces or obedience to parental direction could be an additional deterrent. Mrs Blackmore of Bridlington in East Yorkshire remembers:

The English serviceman, mostly Air Force from the pilot-training area ('erks', with white flashes in their caps) . . . were an added bonus to us in our early twenties. They were fresh, clean-looking fellows and in those days our 'code of conduct' was easy to follow. 'No' meant 'No' and all were friends. Then the Americans swarmed in. They had often 'just flown in' and were prepared to sweep us females off our feet, but they didn't find it that easy. We girls found it better if we went around in a group or at least in twos – though I must say that when I was caught alone, they were, in general, very courteous and anxious not to transgress. Mostly they were homesick and just wanting a few comforts, but I was still too young and wary to extend any hospitality or invitations. We were always very suspicious of females who had lovely Jacqmar scarves and nylon stockings. We reckoned they were a bit fast and were hob-nobbing a little too freely.

Yet the generosity of the Americans was also appreciated. Much was given sincerely, in recognition of the hardship endured by Britain at a time when there were shortages and no rationing on the other side of the Atlantic. At parties and dances thrown by the Americans there always seemed to be unimaginable quantities of cakes, chocolates, ice-cream and pop, as well as things that were even more precious to the adults – fresh coffee and spirits. The children were

Troops helping with the harvest at Lulsgate Bottom, near Bristol, in September 1941.

American airman from the U.S. Air Force base at Mildenhall in Suffolk walks out with local girl.

showered with gifts of sweets, chewing gum or fresh oranges, while adults received cigarettes and perhaps canned food or even a top-up of 'gas'. But there was a darker side to rural Anglo-American relations. Wide boys and spivs were quick to seize an opportunity, and a black-market trade developed with some American camps, where those inside were interested in making a fast buck by providing a wide range of scarce goods to people with the right contacts outside.

Camp commanders were instructed to keep their troops under control and to cultivate a friendly relationship with the Limeys. In general, the Americans were very conscious of their image and good at public relations, in repairing the monuments their tanks knocked down in negotiating narrow streets, attending local functions and fêtes, organising children's treats and maybe giving a sizeable donation to the local cottage hospital. Most of them liked Britain, even if living standards seemed unbelievably backward and everything was on such a small scale. 'Gee, to think we crossed the Atlantic to see this' became a popular refrain elicited by each new example of Britain's architectural heritage or native eccentricity. As Barbara Wilcox remarked, 'We forgave them the hedges they drove through and the walls they knocked down and the thunder of their lorries and trucks on our quiet roads. When they left us we missed them. We wished them all the best of luck.' The country people were mindful of the fact that the Americans, like all the Allied forces, were here to fight the Nazis. Mrs Blackmore remembers that:

We had our sad moments – of course – the fellow one had danced with the night before had 'gone for a Burton' the next day. Our farm was a mock aerodrome to deflect bombers away from the nearby Coastal Command air base. An American bomber did lose its engines one day and crashed across our main entrance road, five gates away, which was tragic as the crew went up in flames and I was there to watch. Later I was questioned by American investigating officers, although I could tell them little.

The North Devon people among whom David St John Thomas lived were strongly pro-American: 'we regarded them as saviours. "Over there, say a prayer" became the regional hymn in the area. We really did regard the Americans as saving our bacon. But there were sighs of relief, too, when the Americans departed, and some single girls left with babies had cause to regret that they had ever come. Whatever reaction the Americans provoked, few country people remained indifferent to their presence.

Liaisons with prisoners of war were much rarer, although the Germans, in particular, could turn the heads of impressionable young girls. Mrs Green of Runfold near Farnham in Surrey remembered 'Gunther Fischer – a really handsome, blond and blue-eyed strong young man,' while Mrs Taylor from Cricket St Thomas in Somerset thought that one of their prisoners was 'very sweet on Ivy, the young maid who was by then 17 and very attractive. He showed her pictures of himself skiing in Austria and would write love letters to her which he would hide in an old gatepost.' Slightly older women might simply feel sorry for them and a bit maternal, like Mrs Taylor, towards 'some very pleasant young men who were obviously missing home as much as our own boys (though there were some arrogant Prussians too).' Most of the prisoners liked to 'take out family photographs to show you, and one cleverly carved about six wooden hens which he assembled on what looked like a table tennis racket, which had strings attached with weights on, and as you moved it in a circular movement the hens would peck. He proudly presented it to John, my son.'

Mrs. Taylor found it hard not to help more than was strictly allowed:

One asked for a bible and I gave him a New Testament which I am sure was against the rules. Another asked for razor blades but this I refused.

German prisoners of war gathering, bunching and weighing early carrots near Ormskirk in Lancashire.

On another occasion I was taking John for a walk to the woods when, on the edge, I saw a man persuasively beckoning and I suddenly remembered that our landlord had prisoners felling trees. I very quickly retreated with John complaining that I hadn't picked the hazel nuts I had promised him we would pick. 'Where are the little nuts? Where are the little nuts?' he repeated as I hastily swung him into my arms and bolted home.

After the war I ventured into the wood and there in the middle was a beautiful Austrian type of hut with carved shutters they had built for themselves.

Barbara Wilcox preferred the Italians for their love of children – 'their pockets were regularly rifled for sweets by young rascals of all ages.' Those billeted with families could also be relied upon to keep infants amused and safe while the mothers were otherwise employed. Indeed, *The Farmer & Stock-breeder* reported in December 1942 that one Italian prisoner-of-war risked his life to save a group of children attacked by an infuriated bull. The Italian 'laid into the animal with a hedge-stake which broke into two.' He was badly gored but later recovered in a Midlands hospital.

On occasion, bad feeling could exist between prisoners and the local community. Thus the Cumberland Farmers Union Executive met in October 1944 to discuss a resolution asking for an after-dark curfew to be imposed on Italians working on farms in the county. Under recently relaxed regulations they could, for instance, visit cinemas in the evening, although they were not allowed to enter public houses. Mr. J.W. Watt complained that this gave them too much liberty. 'These Italians finish work at about 4.00 but need not be indoors till 10 o'clock. They roam about the country roads and are a nuisance. Women in lonely districts are nervous about going out at night.'

An even greater menace was thought to be the lack of control over so-called 'non-cooperators' (POWs known to have Nazi sympathies) towards the end of the war. They worked under military escort and should have been confined to camp after their spell of duty. Despite the Minister of Agriculture's assurances in the House of Commons in November 1944 that discipline was adequate, the MP for South West Norfolk, Mr Somerset de Chair, protested:

You are completely misinformed. Those fascists who boasted that they would march through the streets of Cairo are strolling about the streets of Swaffham to the annoyance of the inhabitants.

As the allied armies achieved more resounding victories, the number of POWs greatly increased. By 1944, the sight of prisoners in their blue overalls with dark green or red patches on them, or sometimes in battledress dyed chocolate, was commonplace. Mrs Joyce Burton whose husband farmed at Allerton Mauleverer in Yorkshire, remembers the new influx including Russians who, willingly or not, had fought on Germany's side:

Although from time to time we had German prisoners-of-war working on the farm my clearest memory is of a few autumn days when we had Russian POWs. This must have been the autumn following D-Day as some authority informed us that these men had been released by our forces as they progressed towards Berlin and because they didn't know what to do with them they were sent to camps in the U.K. We were lifting potatoes and booked our POWs through the W.A.E.C. office in Knaresborough and the coach dropped off several Germans at the end of the drive. Then, one day, without warning the usual little gang were replaced by Russians. We noticed they didn't appear to have the usual packed lunch with them. My

Some of the thousands of Russian prisoners of war who had worked or fought for the Germans on the western front and were helping on the land in Lincolnshire and Yorkshire by November 1944.

This photograph of German prisoners of war still working in the Midlands early in 1946 was published in *The Farmers Weekly* with the caption, 'German prisoners are good workers, and on that score should be fed officially to enable them to work hard.'

mother phoned the W.A.E.C. office and was assured that they had been given packed lunches. Soon a neighbour's wife phoned a similar observation, plus the information that the army driver said the men had eaten their lunch on the outward journey – i.e. immediately after breakfast. I was driving a tractor and potato spinner, the Russians were picking the potatoes into baskets and emptying them into the horse-drawn two wheeled carts for hauling to the clamp being built by the foreman. I still remember my shock and concern at seeing these men eating raw swedes from the next field and scouring the hedge for blackberries. Later we realised they had reached

the U.K. only a very short time before that morning and having been on a low diet for so long it was some time before they could return to normal appetite. Meanwhile my mother and our neighbour's wife had consulted and decided that they must do something to help these poor chaps and each day managed to produce something extra for them at the mid-day meal break, such as quantities of jacket potatoes and large rice puddings – we must still have been able to buy some rice with our 'points' and as we had a house-cow there would be plenty of milk. We invited them to eat in the wash-house (which had a table and chairs) and was across a small yard from the back kitchen door. I washed up here after our family meal before rushing back to the potato field – returning their crockery, the Russians demonstrated their thanks by immediately picking up the tea towel and helping me. It seemed to us that these men were either very young (by sign language and writing in the soil we established that one was only 17) or much older than the average British soldier. They used to sing a sad sounding song in the dusk, when waiting for the coach to take them back to camp. One who had a few phrases of English (he said that he was an opera singer) made us understand that they did not wish to be repatriated. At the time we did not appreciate the terror this must have held for them and it's only in recent years that the public have known the sad result of the action of the government of that time in returning them to the U.S.S.R.

Most of the prisoners had to wait for some time after the war for repatriation. In 1946, Mr T. Hartman was posted to a prison camp on Chepstow race course and was put in charge of prisoners billeted on farms in that area:

A German clerk really did all the paperwork, I was merely a figure-head. The camp was run to a high standard of discipline. The prisoners – many of whom had been in the U.S.A. – were really very industrious and on the farms I saw, there was nothing but praise for them; they were very hard workers and became fond of the farm children. I heard of no cases of any trouble with local women and in the months I was there came across no real complaints. I think the prisoners were really glad to be back to civilian life and work and apart from being naturally hard workers, they went out to show they were proud to be German. They received a small wage, and cigarettes were the main currency for any favours they did. They were much more highly regarded than the Italians who had worked on the farms previously. I have thought since that this was a little unfair, as I have come across Italians who were good workers. Quite a few Germans stayed for years after the war and got on well with the local people.

After Chepstow Tony Hartman moved to another camp near Bridgend in Glamorgan. He found this a particularly interesting experience:

All the prisoners there were generals or admirals, except for the few who cooked and were batmen etc. Of course the generals did no work and I used to take them for walks. They signed a parole to say that they would not try to escape, and they enjoyed the countryside. The camp (called Island Farm) was mentioned on the television recently, but the programme was incorrect regarding a break-out from the camp. It happened while the war was still on and the camp was occupied by other ranks at the time. They dug a tunnel from one of the huts under the fence and quite a number got out. They timed it to disrupt our troops who were engaged in the invasion alert; all were recaptured within a short time. Where the tunnel started they had hung pictures of nude girls to distract our guards when they searched the huts.

114

Bored with prison life, General Eisenbeck, Admiral Brauning and General von Boltenstern, inmates of the Island Farm camp, near Bridgend in Glamorgan, help at their own request to harvest oats on a local farm in August 1946.

In fact, few prisoners tried to escape in the early days of the war, expecting that the invasion of Britain would succeed. But as events began to turn against Germany and hopes of being liberated faded, more men made the attempt. Only a handful managed to get any distance: Britain was as much an island fortress for fugitives trying to get out as it was for invaders trying to get in.

Now and again, a brave attempt was foiled by a countryman. Mr Don Davis, a well-known Herefordshire farmer and stockbreeder, was the central figure in the recapture of an Italian POW in July 1943. The man jumped from a fast-moving express train in which he was travelling under escort to a military hospital. After rolling down an embankment and getting a severe shaking in the process, he was seen making off towards an orchard, whereupon two men working there ran for Mr Davis, a special constable, who made the arrest.

With the end of the war, most of the strangers in the village sooner or later returned to their own homes or homelands, once more to pick up the main thread of their lives. A few either stayed on or returned to marry locally and become respected and useful members of the rural community, although for a while they would still be regarded as foreigners whether they came from Liverpool, Leipzig or St Louis.

Chapter 4
A RIFLE AND 60 ROUNDS IN THE WARDROBE

The deluge of leaflets about home defence that landed on the nation's doormats in the summer of 1939 included one or two that were not exactly what they seemed at first sight. Among them were unofficial items in which the letters ARP did not mean Air Raid Precautions but Awake! Repent! Prepare! By this time the usual meaning of the initials had been embodied in such a blast of press coverage and government propaganda that even the most isolated inhabitant of the countryside could hardly have avoided some sense of disaster to be averted and some recognition of public duty.

The depths of the countryside were thought to be safer than most places because it stood to reason that the Germans were not going to waste perfectly good bombs on remote farms. Nevertheless, the more responsible country households rubbed up on their knowledge of first aid and gas precautions, dug an air-raid shelter and prepared to receive refugees, sometimes to the amusement of their less responsible neighbours. Black-out instructions were sent out in July 1939: where ordinary curtains were not thick or heavy enough to meet official requirements, 'a length of opaque black cloth might be hung on a rod and supported by cup-hooks across the entire window-embrasure,

A spirited attempt at camouflage of what looks like a country cinema, photographed on 3rd September 1939.

Cord and Eyelet Blinds.

Lancaster Blindcloth for screens.

NATIONAL *and a* DOMESTIC DUTY

Look to your windows. Are they safe, are they bright? Make this resolution — do away with window mourning and dangerous makeshifts — Fix simple blinds which never show a chink of light by night, but disappear by day. Get back to lovely drapings and welcome the summer sun into your homes. Be safe but bright.

Your local retailer will supply you with LANCASTER BLINDCLOTH, complying with Government A.R.P. requirements, for home-made "screens", etc.

Insist on LANCASTER BLINDCLOTH.

● **Cord and Eyelet Blinds.** This simple but ingenious design is the cheapest type of cord-operated drop, consisting of flat wood slat at top for nailing to window frame, and a plain round wood pole at the bottom with a cord passing through eyelets for raising blind from bottom to top; the blind rolling up with the round pole.

● **Lancaster Blindcloth** is an excellent material for "screens" made at home. It is simple to handle and will last for years.

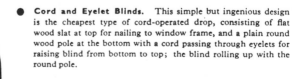

LANCASTER *Blindcloth*
Jas. Williamson & Son, Limited, Lancaster

Advertisement in *Illustrated*, 20th April 1940.

or used to line curtains.' By 26th September, Countrywoman's column in *The Farmer & Stock-breeder* reported that all stocks of black-out material had been exhausted. Much ingenuity went into finding substitutes, although the really prudent had kept tucked away in their drawer a reserve of 'Government-spaced linen' a dingy brown material produced in World War I as a defence against Zeppelin attack.

Making a tent in an anti-aircraft emplacement in Kent look like a haystack, 1st September 1939.

Windows had to be reinforced against bomb splinters, another 'tedious and ticklish procedure' as Countrywoman remarked:

I have wrestled with adhesive nets. It took me the best part of two afternoons to cover those twenty-four squares in a north window . . . Towards the end I somewhat quickened up the job by reinforcing the mucilage supplied on the net with an adhesive recommended by ARP experts – a good, clear gum to which has been added a sixth part of glycerine . . . To the small windows in the narrow hall we have attached wire pea-guards, staggered in two layers to lessen the resulting mesh. Larger sheets of wire-netting or Cellophane attached with the gum-glycerine aforementioned account for the rest of the windows.

Now that war had broken out, air raids seemed imminent enough and more people started wanting to construct shelters. Sometimes the materials that came to hand were not too promising – *The Farmers Weekly* reported on 15th September that villagers in East Anglia were cutting out shelters in corn stacks. Many country people, like those in towns, thought that they could manage by sheltering under the stairs, bringing down a spare mattress, pillows and blankets to ensure a degree of comfort. Anyway, in areas that had been designated as safe, government shelters were difficult to obtain. A farmer in the Eastern Counties reported to *The Farmer & Stock-breeder* on 16th July 1940:

In a nearby railway siding two truck loads of Anderson shelters had been standing for three months. Here, I thought, was just the thing. The shelters were obviously not wanted and they would answer admirably if placed at handy spots throughout the farm.

But the rejoinder of the Ministry of Home Security was that the shelters could not be bought by farmers. Those in question were evidently being diverted elsewhere, said the official. This raised the speculation that, if it takes Sir John Anderson's department 3 months to divert shelters, there must be something wrong!

Getting a local builder to construct a home-made shelter was not necessarily a simple task, as a farmer's wife discovered:

We are going to have an air raid shelter. The builder has done his best to dissuade us, trying to show how no one could live in a safer place than we. But we told him how useful it would be after the war, converted into a bathroom; and Harold said how much safer the wife would feel (these men are never frightened?), and I said how nice it would be to feel the children were safe sleeping in the shelter; and the bricklayer said, in his amused friendly voice (this was all over the telephone) 'Why, the war'll be over by the time we've got it built. What then?'

Anti-aircraft unit in readiness for the enemy.

More elaborate precautions were needed for important buildings. A government leaflet in September 1939 urged owners of country houses to keep fire-fighting equipment on the top floor, after clearing out attics and roof-spaces of 'accumulated junk'. Treasures were to be well packed in wooden boxes and monuments boarded and protected with sandbags filled with the driest possible sand – damp might do as much damage as bombs. Parsons were to ensure the safety of their churches by providing fire-fighting materials and by organising a volunteer fire-party. Another pamphlet noted that movable effects – plate, books, vestments and paintings – could be removed to a storage place provided by the Diocesan Advisory Committee, but that the removal of precious old glass should be attempted only by a properly skilled glazier. The almost impossible task of blacking out the church windows was resolved by reverting to the old practice of bringing forward Sunday evening services to 3 o'clock in the afternoon during winter months.

The black-out made the roads much more dangerous. All vehicle lights had to be masked, though exactly how and when was difficult to work out from the flood of conflicting regulations, orders and counter-orders. Road casualty figures soared, with the monthly total of adult pedestrian pedestrians killed more than tripling between August and September, from 168 to 550. On narrow roads, a top speed of 15 m.p.h. was recommended, and even on main roads it was not thought safe to drive at more than 30 m.p.h.

Some local authorities and organisations added strange regulations of their own. The New Forest Commoners Defence Association, for instance, appealed in September for pony owners to keep their animals on enclosed land 'or if they must pasture them on common land, as they are entitled to do, animals should be marked with paint, making white stripes on their hind quarters and in the position of the saddle girth.' Motorists confronted after dark with these home-grown zebras must have wondered if they were seeing things.

Other lighting regulations seemed senselessly irritating. Farmers carting hay after dark became liable to prosecution as hay and straw were on the list of inflammable materials that were banned from public roads at night. A farmer at Camborne in Cornwall was prosecuted for this offence in January 1940 but was discharged on payment of costs. A less fortunate offender from Butlers Marston in Warwickshire was fined 20s (with costs) for taking cows along the road after dark without a shaded light at front and rear, while, in what was described as a most unusual case, a Scottish farmer was reprimanded at Campbeltown Sheriff's Court in Argyllshire in March 1940 for having used a horse-drawn cart on the road during the black-out without having both ends of the vehicle painted white.

Air-raid precautions on the farm. Left: galvanised iron being put in position over a dairy window to provide a virtually gas-proof screen and well as giving some protection from blast and serving as black-out. Below: demonstrating how a bleach mixture would be used on a horse affected by blister gas.

Country baker Harold Castell goes on working in November 1940 just as he has done for 25 years, but with a change of headgear.

A cartoon in *The Land Worker* in August 1940 suggests another use for a gas-mask.

Much less of a joke was the threat of a gas attack. From the summer of 1939, the civilian population was instructed in the recognition of blister gases such as mustard gas or Yperite (called after Ypres which had been the scene of some of the fiercest fighting in World War I) or those of the choking variety – phosgene and chlorine. Gas-masks were to be carried everywhere outdoors, slung over the shoulder in their awkward square boxes. Only the most reckless chose to go without, but others sought a more convenient receptacle, whether a haversack, an old camera case, or even granny's discarded knitting bag. All that mattered was that it should be waterproof, light and unobtrusive.

Animals, too, could be at risk from gas, and on 1st September 1939 *The Farmers Weekly* recommended:

In 'danger areas' animal housing can be made fairly gasproof by closing the windows and doors, and hanging plenty of sacking or blankets, saturated with water, over them. All air outlets should be blocked. Protection from flying splinters and glass may be provided by sandbagging the buildings up to a height of about 6 feet. Damage from glass is made less likely if laths or netting are nailed across windows. Land that has been contaminated by gas must be kept absolutely clear of animals for at least 3 weeks.

The most dangerous gases are mustard and Lewisite, both liquid gases. Animals which have been splashed by these gases should be wiped clean with a rag or cotton wool treated with petrol or paraffin; bleach ointment should then be rubbed in and wiped off after 5 minutes, after which the body should be covered with a paste made of bleaching powder and water. Eyes should be treated with a solution consisting of one teaspoonful of bicarbonate of soda to a pint of water. The authorities suggest that farmers should make a point of becoming acquainted with the nearest air-raid warden, whose advice may be invaluable.

To deal with the possibility of animals being caught in bombing raids when in transit or in urban markets, an animal A.R.P. corps was established. The initiative was taken by the Glasgow and West of Scotland Veterinary College during the first months of the war, when 70 students enrolled in a scheme that was intended to prevent a stampede of horses and cattle at markets in the Glasgow area. The idea was soon taken up elsewhere and by November some 2,000

Above: a team of animal A.R.P. workers, including butchers, cattlemen and grooms, led by a vet, at West Bromwich in Birmingham in October 1940. Left: an animal A.R.P guard registering a cow and issuing it with an identity disc on a farm in Essex in November 1939 as part of a national scheme to register all the country's farm animals.

animal guards had been appointed nationally, their tasks including the issuing of identity disks for animals in case they strayed during a raid.

During the winter months, the attack from the skies failed to materialise. The phoney war ended, however, in the spring of 1940, and the first civilian to be killed in an air raid was a countryman, James Isbister, a farmer's son from Orkney. His story was told emotively in *Illustrated* magazine on 20th April.

This is the simple story of the life and death of James Isbister, of the Parish of Stenness, in the Orkneys.

It ends at the age of 27, when a German bomb made him the first civilian to die in an air raid on British soil in the Nazi War.

He had not gone to war, war came to him. It found him suddenly on a moonlight night on the threshold of his own home. Out of the sky rained bombs upon an obscure hamlet called the Bridge of Waith.

It found him going to succour a woman neighbour whose house had collapsed in ruins. It killed him within a few feet of his wife and three months old baby.

Thus an unknown German airman, in the wantonness of modern war, destroyed an unknown road labourer.

Sardonic fate mocked when it chose James Isbister even as a footnote of history or an item in the stop-press of the newspapers.

By the early summer, there was further loss of in the countryside, although most often the destruction was restricted to buildings and a few stock. Thus *The Farmers Weekly* reported during the last week of June that a German plane had heavily bombed a farm 'in an Eastern County'. 'Evidently,' it noted with sarcasm, 'the pilot thought that a hayrick on the farm was an important objective, for after dropping bombs on it he came down low and blazed away at it with his machine-guns. But the people at the farm had taken refuge and the only casualties were a few sheep.'

S.O. Ratcliff who farmed around Maldon near the Essex coast wished that he were further from the enemy:

I think many of them who think home is the safest place just shoot out their bombs in my area and bolt . . . We had a wonderful case of this once when the enemy had evidently got thoroughly frightened and unloaded some 250 incendiaries and 50 H.E. on one of the farms. Our men rushed about picking up the fire-stcks off the sheds and stacks, and a lot more dropped on the cornfields. We estimated that damage at about £1, and I am glad to say that practically no one was hurt.

Cattle graze in a field near the coast in May 1940 as barbed wire barriers are put in position.

In August, the Battle of Britain was at its peak and raged in the air over the south-eastern counties. Labourers working in the fields had a ringside seat for the aerial combat and would cheer RAF attacks on incoming enemy aircraft. Major Jarvis reported in *Country Life*:

Last week, when there were some light fine-weather clouds floating about in the clear evening sky, I came across a party of timber-men watching a series of fights from their stance on a lofty pile of pine logs.

'He'll get that fellow all right!' someone shouted. 'Look! He's coming right down on his tail. Hear the machine-guns now!'

There was a faint stuttering of fire from the northern horizon and a long-drawn 'Aaaah' from the crowd – the sound one heard in other days when a rocket at a fire display came to earth in a shower of sparks – and a light grey German plane shot downwards until it disappeared behind a belt of trees.

'Got him!' roared the crowd. 'Down and out. Look there's our chap going over him to check up,' as the tiny British machine swooped downwards over the spot. Then as a dense column of black smoke went drifting away to the eastwards the little Spitfire zoomed up again.

'He's after another now – good boy. Look!'

A second German machine appeared overhead speeding southwards, and roaring behind him and overtaking him as if he were standing still came the British machine, black against the evening sky.

'Damn it, the swine will be in that cloud before our chap gets on his tail. No, he won't. Yes, he will. Hard luck – they ought to have what you might call a forward gun to stop anything breaking cover ahead. And, by God, they have – there's another of ours in front of him. There go the guns again. Aaah!' – And coming down in irregular spiral with smoke pouring from its tail came a second Junker bomber.

'Not bad for ten minutes,' said the commentator laconically, 'and if I am not mistaken they got a third one while we were watching the second scrap. Now I am going home to supper, and I'll sleep sound and contented tonight.'

Acts of heroism by country people began to be reported. In July 1940, Gerald Winter, a foreman ploughman from Peacehaven in Sussex was awarded the medal of the Order of the British Empire, Civil Division, for gallantry in rescuing one of the crew of an RAF Blenheim aircraft that crashed and caught fire at Jeffries Point, Portslade. A week later, a farmer's wife from north-eastern England, Mrs Norman Cardwell, received the same award. A German airman whose 'plane had been shot down landed by parachute near her home. Mrs Cardwell walked up to him and told him to put his hands up. She then took his revolver and marched behind him to the road, where he was later handed over to the police and soldiers. Mrs Cardwell's courage was said to have appealed so much to Winston Churchill that he cut all red tape and had the award announced within 24 hours.

On his own ground, the countryman was not easily intimidated by coming up against the enemy at first hand. *The Farmers Weekly* published a story on 1st November 1940 which it assured its readers was true:

Down in the West County the crew of a Nazi aircraft baled out and fell in open country. The first person one of them encountered was a rather ancient cowman on his way to get in the cows for the morning milking.

The airman in excellent English said: 'I am a German officer and I wish to be taken prisoner.'

To which the cowman replied without hesitation: 'I can't bother wi' thee now. Thee come along of I an' get in they cows, and then we'll see about thee.'

Meanwhile, the growing number of Land Girls now working in the battle areas were carrying on bravely even under heavy fire. *The Farmers Weekly* reported on 3rd December:

In Kent over 200 have worked on steadily in constant danger. Six of them have been doing tractor ploughing in a particularly dangerous coastal barrage area. It is not 'done' to shelter until the battle is overhead – otherwise one would be forever sheltering.

The tractors were so noisy that the drivers could not tell when the battle was overhead. So frequently they found themselves working with shrapnel falling all round them and even on their tractors. Not one of these girls asked for a transfer. Instead they applied for steel helmets – and got them!

On one front-line farm in Kent, the livestock losses included 40 sheep and a five-year-old cart mare worth £70. In one piece of pasture there were 93 bomb-holes, one of them 40 feet across, which filled with water to a depth of 20 feet. The farmer's son commented 'As a break from bombing we sometimes get machine-gunning. That is definitely not so healthy. We had just left off threshing the other day when one blighter came hurtling down to 150 feet and sprayed us. We threw ourselves under a wagon just in time.'

The hazards of working in the countryside added to other factors to reduce the number of Londoners taking their traditional holiday hop-picking. To cope with the labour shortage, some 2,000 soldiers were drafted in to harvest the crops and Kent Education Committee suspended school attendance rules, freeing any children who wanted to join the pickers. On a visit to 'Messrs. Whitbread's famous hop yard in the heart of Kent', for a correspondent *The Farmers Weekly* was impressed by the preparations:

Digging trenches for the Kent hop-pickers to shelter in during air-raids, August 1940.

A celebrated image of the war: children helping with the Kentish hop harvest, said to be watching an aerial dog fight from the shelter of a trench. It was published in *The Farmer's Weekly* in the early autumn of 1940 and eventually made the cover of *Life* magazine where 'it told the people of the United States what life in wartime was like for our children in Britain. It has taken their story around the world.' It was published again in *The Farmers Weekly* in 1945 in celebration of VE Day with a lengthy quotation from Psalm 147 ('The Lord lifteth up the meek: he casteth the wicked down to the ground . . .').

Over a quarter of a mile of trenches have been dug in readiness for the 900 families who will descend on the gardens at the end of August. This has meant two months of toil by men earning 12s 6d a day, a heavy drain on any farmer's pocket. Every advantage has been taken of the natural surroundings to hide the shelters from the air. More than half of them have been dug under a clump of large oak trees while others are in a corner of the hop fields.

At the two encampments near the farm, casualty stations have been built, and these are equipped with first-aid outfits and stretchers. Here it is planned that slight casualties should be treated, while in case of serious injury stretcher-bearers will carry the patient to a temporary hospital inside the farm building. A doctor is to be in charge of the hospital.

A visit to the oasts and buildings showed that they were equally well protected. Twelve fire hydrants and over 1,500 feet of hose can be brought into play should incendiary bombs fall on the long sloping roof. I noticed that the white cowls have been painted black this year, and was told that they were thought to be too conspicuous from the air. Some of the buildings, too, have been camouflaged, but for the most part the appearance of this landmark farm in the Weald of Kent remains unaltered.

The precautions against air raids were not allowed to interfere with the normal business of harvesting more than was absolutely necessary. Nevertheless, in the background lurked constant anxiety about the possibility of an enemy invasion. At first, the military defence of the rural counties was undertaken by regular troops. They could be found billeted in the villages, and their vehicles patrolled the lanes. With the launch of the German defensive in Spring 1940, the situation changed. Fear of airborne invasion and of secret treachery by fifth columnists led to the setting up of a home militia that could be mobilised to cope with local emergencies. The call to join the Local Defence Volunteers was broadcast by the Secretary of State for War, Sir Anthony Eden, on 14th May 1940. Men between the ages of 17 and 65 of reasonable fitness and with a knowledge of firearms were asked to give in their names at the local police station. The response was immediate and overwhelming: a quarter of a million enrolled within 24 hours. As A.G. Smith commented in his book *From Dusk to Dawn* published in 1943:

There was no doubt that the rapid worsening of the war situation in France was one reason for this, but the major one was that this new volunteer force provided an opportunity for thousands of men to feel that at last they could do something to help their country in her hour of need. Ex-soldiers, considered too old for fighting could show that they were not too old. Lads of 17 and middle-aged civilians could show that they were as good as the old soldiers. Civilians of military age who had been prevented from joining the service by reason of the value of their civilian work could now give their scanty leisure to training as part time soldiers. Civilians, and there were many, who never before shouldered a Service rifle and who hated the enemy and all its works, could now fall in with the others, and in so doing, forget some of their prejudices and many of their fears.

Countrywomen, used to hunting and shooting, came forward as well, but a large proportion of the half million people who had joined the L.D.V. by mid-June were veterans of World War I. The main task of the L.D.V. was to look out for, report and if necessary delay enemy parachutists. There were doubts, though, about the ability of the new force to deal with a determined, highly trained and mobile enemy. It seemed ludicrous that the L.D.V., equipped with shot-guns, a share of a rifle, or even more primitive weapons – Lord Croft advocated that the pike might still be used to advantage 'to pin down the enemy' – could stand up to the modern arsenal possessed by the Wehrmacht. Major Jarvis disagreed:

Those who served in the Boer War know that many an advance was held up, many a gun put out of action, and many a grave dug in the veldt, through the very straight shooting of septuagenarian and even octogenerian snipers armed with aged sporting rifles: and the arms of precision in the British Army of those days – the Maxim, Colt and Lea-Metford rifle – were not so very much inferior to the weapons in use today . . .

The big-game shooter's 'ball and cartridge' gun, with the barrel slightly rifled at the muzzle, is effective with ball ammunition up to 200 yards, the ordinary unrifled gun up to about half that range, the considerable margin of error being probably due to lack of adequate sighting. For this reason cartridges with BB or SSG loads may be more deterrent; buckshot, though heavier, are fewer and therefore less reliable. In the absence of anything else, an ordinary cartridge cut in half across the wad makes quite a formidable projectile, as the shot scatters very little.

Three weeks later, Major Jarvis was able to report on the recommissioning of elderly firearms for use by the L.D.V. and was inspired to some characteristically blimpish musings:

The busiest man in the village is the gunsmith, who with his staff is working overtime repairing shot-guns, sporting rifles, and those illegal relics of the last war that returning warriors brought home with them in defiance of orders. Most of us regret now that we were so modest in being satisfied with one rifle, and we admire the large ideas of the man who has unearthed an old Lewis gun complete with a pan of ammunition.

Considering that a goodly proportion of our members have spent much of their time abroad, there is a disappointing shortage of sporting rifles and revolvers, and this would appear to be due to the rather pettyfogging regulations concerning firearms that pertain in this country in ordinary times. One serves 20 years or more abroad, and the whole of that time one is entrusted with a veritable arsenal of weapons – in fact, I recall a period when we received direct orders that if we happened to be assassinated when not wearing a revolver we would be punished by the withholding of compensation from our next-of-kin.

Immediately one steps into this country, however, one is treated as a potential murderer, gunman or suicide, and retention of one's arms means constant worry with licences and visits from the police . . .

The call for shot-guns has had an immediate and most satisfactory response in our part of the world, but we are not quite certain yet if a licence is necessary for German parachutists or not. One can hardly regard them as feathered or ground game, and one imagines there is no close season; but, on the other hand, free shooting has never been recognised in any part of the British Isles, and the Government does not make exception even in the case of vermin. The other day, when I wished to add to my firearm licence a sporting Mannlicher, lent me by a friend for the parachutist season, I was called upon to pay 2s 6d before anything could be done about it, and the transfer is not completed yet.

The organisation of the L.D.V. went ahead with commendable speed. On the coast line of Kent and Sussex, where the danger was greatest, patrols went on look-out duty before the end of the first day of recruitment. Elsewhere things took a little longer, but only in

The first cavalry troop of the Local Defence Volunteers, formed by Devon farmers, patrols Exmoor in the summer of 1940 to guard against German parachute landings.

a few areas in the invasion zone was there any serious delay.

During the summer of 1940, a few mounted units were recruited, usually from members of the local hunt. The Exmoor troop was one of the earliest, while another – the York troop of 50 volunteers – was organised by Squadron Leader W. Thompson, ex-sheriff of York, a farmer and keen rider to hounds. The troop's job was to patrol one hundred square miles of the North Riding of Yorkshire, *Illustrated* featured the troop in its issue of 7th September 1940:

No one who could not ride expertly and shoot to sporting standard stood the smallest chance of becoming a member of the squadron. Once formed the squadron immediately began dawn and dusk patrols, cavalry saddles and equipment were issued to the volunteers, as were rifles and revolvers.

Being so mobile and independent of roads, the 'Mounties' are able to race to any point under observation in the shortest possible time, added to which their marksmanship when shooting and knowledge of locality, will make them a deadly menace to any invader.

One of the L.D.V.'s responsibilities was to keep a continuous check for subversive activities, and after the evacuation of Dunkirk, wild stories about spies abounded. One rumour was that German paratroopers disguised as nuns were going to drop from the skies with weapons concealed beneath their billowing habits. This story could be traced back to a report by the Dutch Foreign Minister at a London press conference in May that saboteurs in unlikely disguises had been dropped into Holland shortly before its invasion. By the summer months, any new face or unfamiliar accent provoked instant suspicion in rural districts, and failure to produce an identity card on demand was likely to mean several hours' detention in the nearest police station.

L.D.V. efforts to keep the country free from subversion could have their irritant qualities, particularly to travellers stopped repeatedly at road blocks. A majority, perhaps, accepted the inconvenience as a tiresome necessity, but the less patient saw it as petty tyranny. They were likely to get short shrift from the Volunteers. A.G. Street

Covered by a colleague, a Local Defence Volunteer checks a driver's papers. For some reason, the car has only one of its headlights masked in the regulation manner.

noted that the motorist who refused to show his identification 'on the grounds that he had already shown it 20 times in the last 30 miles and swore at those who now demanded it, found his car key extracted, his car pushed to one side of the road, and his person held until the civil police took over and gave him the necessary reprimand.'

From May 1940, the Government had to prepare the civilian population for the possibility of invasion. The main instruction was to stay put and keep out of the way of the military, especially making sure not to venture on to the roads and risk holding up troops on their way to the front. Motorists were to immobilise their cars by locking them in their garages and removing the distributor arm as well as the ignition key.

Farmers were to help deter invasion by placing obstacles in fields that might be used as landing sites. One man in the Midlands was reported as setting his ricks out in his field in such a manner that 'even an autogiro could have a job to land there', while others in North Lincolnshire proved even more inventive by putting their manure around the fields in small heaps rather than in large heaps in the corners, an expedient which had already proved useful in dousing incendiary fires.

If invasion actually occurred, the government's instructions were to go on producing food until military action made this impossible. Dairy cows had still to be milked and farmers were expected to train other members of their households to milk efficiently because the regular milkers who were members of the L.D.V. might be otherwise occupied. As road and rail transport were likely to be dislocated, milk, fruit and vegetables should be sold or given away to British troops. Tractors were to be immobilised, and men, horses and stock to be kept off public roads.

In the coastal area north of the Humber, civilian patrols were trained in the use of explosives and firearms by Auxiliary Units from the East Yorkshire Regiment. Each patrol had a subterranean hide-out constructed, usually in a wood, by the Royal Engineers. If invasion loomed, they were supposed to take ammunition and a week's supply of food and lie low. Then, when the area was occupied, they would emerge to harass the enemy with guerilla tactics.

In July 1940 the government reorganised the L.D.V. and gave it a new name suggested by the Prime Minister: the Home Guard. Up to this stage, the organisation of the L.D.V. had been pretty informal: many platoons were formed after a summons to the squire's library, a meeting in the village hall or the tap room of the local pub. Leadership was often assumed by the local squire or some other worthy, but ranks were otherwise kept to a minimum and more or less the only uniforms were a few that were taken out of mothballs and struggled into after a space of twenty years or so. The spirit of the L.D.V. was

John Kingdon Ward, the author's father, a civil engineer with the Admiralty, who joined the Home Guard in 1940, when this photograph was taken.

130

of cheerful nostalgia amongst old comrades, glad to be back in harness, but not as yet subject to any real military discipline or rigorous training.

By the beginning of August, the job was being taken more seriously, and the War Office had grouped the new Home Guard units into battalions and zones. The battalions were given county titles and greater liaison was envisaged with their counterparts in the army.

Before the changes were fully assimilated, the Home Guard had to face its first major alert. In the late summer of 1940, Hitler decided to switch the main impact of the bombing away from the military targets and on to Britain's cities. The Blitz began with an all-night raid on London on 23rd August, followed by another on 7th September which the Chiefs of Staff considered was the clear prelude to invasion itself. The Home Forces were put on immediate alert with the code word Cromwell. This meant that troops were to take up battle stations and ready themselves for an early engagement with the enemy. The result was much confusion, as the code word was widely interpreted as meaning that the German troops had already landed on British beaches. Church bells, silent since the beginning of the war, rang out across the countryside. The Home Guard mobilised, as did air-raid wardens, police and everyone else associated with civil defence – the civilian population stayed at home and waited.

One of four pictures published on a page of *The Field* on 29th June 1940. Under the heading, an instruction to 'Cut this page out and hang it up,' the text stated, 'The War Office has asked us to publish these pictures of German Troop Carriers to help you to distinguish the enemy. Take a piece of cardboard and stick this page on it and hang it in a prominent place.' The picture is of a Junkers JU. 52 with BMW engines, 'the most important German troop-carrier, and the one normally used for parachute dropping.'

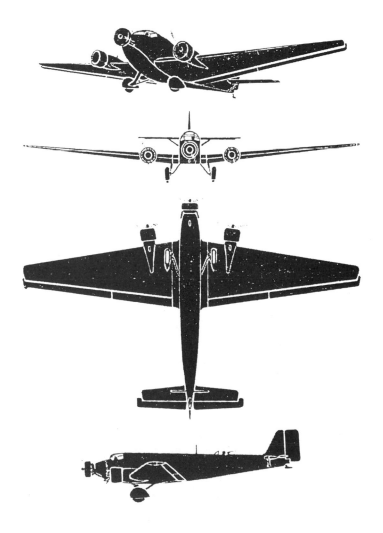

A shepherd and his flock pass a wrecked German aircraft brought down by British fighters near the south coast, 7th September 1940.

Through the long, warm night of 7th September, the defenders remained standing-to. Arthur Street, on his way back to Wiltshire after broadcasting in London, found them 'round every bend and at every crossroad with loaded rifles and itching fingers.' Dawn brought little relief, and the situation was not clarified until noon. Even so, the alert continued for another fortnight, bringing further alarms and excursions. Stephen Pratt of Twyford in Berkshire recalled:

It had been agreed that in the event of an invasion church bells would be rung to give a good alarm. One night in the small hours, I was on patrol outside with a fellow member (a farm worker) when he suddenly grabbed my arm and said 'Mr Pratt! Mr Pratt!' (Christian names were not exactly in common use then) 'Invasion!' After my initial surprise I was able to point out to him that the bells we could hear were not church bells but the postmaster's chiming clock.

The general degree of apprehension can be gauged from another panic that occurred on Saturday, 23rd September, one of those lovely days in the south of England, when summer passes into autumn. As *The Field* recounted in November:

The early morning fields glistened with millions of single spider-silk threads, later to rise and float away in the rising air current as the dew evaporated with the heat of the sun. Although not a rare phenomenon, those gossamer threads caused much concern to the military high command, who suspected them of having been sown by enemy aircraft and of being poisonous. An urgent warning was issued to Home Guard detachments in the southern county, much to the amusement of local countrymen . . .

As autumn wore on, the threat of invasion receded, although the Home Guard continued to have a go at the Luftwaffe. One unit in the South Eastern Command was credited with having brought down an enemy plane by rifle fire – no mean achievement even though the aircraft would have been flying very low. A more common excitement was the opportunity to apprehend an enemy airman who had been forced to bale out. A.G. Street recalled:

One dark night about ten o'clock, just as I was going upstairs to bed, I received a message by telephone to the effect that a German airman who baled out some days before had been seen some seven miles away. So I grabbed greatcoat, gum-boots and arms and in a few minutes had the cross roads blocked by half a dozen men, and two car-loads scouting up different roads.

In perhaps a dozen neighbouring villages other Home Guards did the same and by eleven o'clock the quarry was captured, unfortunately not by my guard. However, a car from a neighbouring platoon reported that the man was now in the local police station so

Another German fighter brought down by the RAF, this time in a Wiltshire cornfield.

Members of the crew of five of a Heinkel 111, shot down by a British Hurricane over the south-east coast when returning from a bombing raid on the London area on 12th September 1940, being marched off under escort from the burning wreckage of their aircraft.

we set off to have a look at him. Incidentally, to see six stalwart Home Guards emerging from a Ford Ten, all complete with rifles and fixed bayonets, is an awe-inspiring sight.

Presently, I joined a mixed company in the local police station that was almost filled to bursting point. There were ten or a dozen Home Guards, three police constables, and one police sergeant busy at the telephone. In the middle was the prisoner, steadily eating bread and butter, while most of us wished that the sergeant would hurry up with his telephoning so we could inquire details of his captive.

The prisoner was a young man about twenty-three, not at all the bogey of so many people's imaginations, but a very ordinary, decent-looking lad. There was a curious dignity about him too, and I wondered whether I should have been able acquit myself so well in a comparable situation in Germany. Frankly, I doubted it very much.

As I was driving home I realised that I, a civilian, had just experienced my first taste of war, and that I disliked it intensely. I was dead keen to hurt the fellow, felt the same exhilaration as I did when

Not all the aircraft brought down were German. This twin-engined Italian bomber is one of seven brought down by an RAF squadron over Suffolk on 11th November 1940. Rammed by the leader of the squadron after his ammunition had run out, the aircraft crashed in a forest near the village of Bromeswell.

hounds were running, and would have shot him on the instant if need be. But, somehow, when he was caught I had no further quarrel with him.

The mass raids of August and September brought fresh horror not only to the city but to country areas as well. On 13th September, *The Farmers Weekly* published a selection of readers' letters on the

The remains of a Messerschmitt 109 shot down on the hills behind Brighton in Sussex on 6th October 1940.

The church flag raised in front of the Church of the Annunciation at Chislehurst in Kent after bombing in 1940.

subject, noting that 'somehow we can't talk of anything else this week but air raids':

Somewhere in Sussex . . . We are finding it increasingly difficult to go far from home these days, as we get some big air battles this way. About a fortnight ago there was a generous dumping of bombs; this Friday there was a bomber brought down within a very short distance. Of course there was the usual stream of sightseers; but some people were sorry that they went, for it was not a pleasant sight – two of the men had come down with the burning 'plane. I *do* feel that it serves people right when they get a shock through being so morbid.

Somewhere in Shropshire . . . So far we have been lucky in the matter of air raids; but the raiders have visited places only a few miles from here. A little to the south-west of us the very quietest rural parishes have been bombed, the least likely region for air raids one would have thought; and there, too, almost no harm has been done, except to the glass porch of a farm house, and a store cupboard where a piece of shrapnel landed in a pot of jam.

The bombing even reached into some areas of Wales, from which one reader wrote to the woman's page editor of *The Farmers Weekly*:

Dear Mrs Day, – I have been thinking about you a lot during these very troublous days, and praying, too, for all the poor people in and around London.

You would hardly believe the bombers would get as far as where we are, but every evening the drone begins and for seven hours the other night it was really awful right around us for miles. We stayed in a dug-out in one of our fields; and for five hours again the next

night. Clusters of incendiary bombs fell on the mountain close to here, fires lighting up the whole countryside almost 10 miles away. For hours the crash of high explosives alternated with fire bombs, most of them falling in open country.

Some of the first bomb damage in Kent: about 30 acres of greenhouses destroyed at Flowerhill Nurseries, Gravesend in July 1940.

One little village near here that suffered severely in a great pit disaster some time ago has now been victim of another kind of tragedy. Quite a lot of damage was done there – many died. It is only a short distance over the fields from here; I keep thinking of the men, women, and children I knew who lost their lives that night.

A farmer on one hillside had a miraculous escape; he survived, though his two sisters and a workman were killed on the same farm.

We seem to be right in the centre of it; bombs and flares falling in the villages all around us. At 2 p.m. one day I was far up the fields, feeding the fowl, when the siren sounded. As I couldn't get as far as our dug-out quick enough, my little dog and I took cover in one of the fowl houses.

Well, dear Mrs Day, I am hoping we shall soon have more cheerful news. For I have noticed this year, on opening the shells of some broad beans that the beans instead of hanging down from the top, are growing upwards from the bottom of the pod. Country people say that when this happens 'a war will end.' Certainly the last time I myself found pods like this was in 1918. So here's hoping the old saying will come true again and we shall have the reptile who has caused all this world chaos by the heels.

I pray God will keep you and yours safe and sound. – A.L.R.

The raids elicited reactions that ranged from genuine fright to calm acceptance or cheerful fatalism. One woman in East Anglia noted that she didn't take any more notice of them than summer thunder storms – they were soon gone. A farmer's wife recalled:

An elderly neighbour said she got up, dressed and walked up and down her room all night. Thinking to prevent her having another restless night, a friend asked if she ever prayed for protection, and received the indignant and affronted reply that she had never prayed more earnestly. 'Then you should have gone quietly to bed, pulled the blankets over your ears, and settled down to sleep' was the confident reply.

One surprisingly effective form of defence against the bombs, as Sir Archibald Hurd found, was Norfolk thatch. He reported on his experience in a letter to *Country Life* on 5th November 1941:

It was early one morning. 'The Battle of Britain' was being fought over our heads. For several hours we had sat in our shelter room. When there was a lull in the proceedings, we decided that, as all fighting was apparently at an end, we would go to bed. This we did and were soon fast asleep. Our awakening was a rude one. At 2 a.m. there were violent explosions; the windows and doors of the house were blown in and the plaster of the ceilings and walls of the bedrooms as well as, so we discovered later, of every other room was shattered into fragments. We instinctively covered our heads with the bed clothes, with the result that none of us was injured.

Three bombs had fallen; one had wrecked a neighbouring cottage, another had missed our house by a split second and a further one had fallen in our woods – several hundred yards away. A German pilot on his way back from London had decided to unload his bombs, probably because he was being chased, and our hillside was as good a place as any other. So the bombs were landed on us while we were in bed and the interior of our home was wrecked. It presented an indescribable scene of ruin – doors, windows, ceilings and walls looked as if they could never be repaired.

I telephoned to an architect who examined the damage. He was satisfied that we probably owed our escape uninjured to the Norfolk thatch, which is over a foot thick. In his opinion it had acted as a cushion when the bombs exploded. A few of the rafters had been split – not broken – but the roof itself had given slightly under the impact, broken the force of the explosion, and then recovered. Some pieces of the metal of the bomb had lodged in the thatch, but

Bomb damage in the village of Eynsford in Kent.

Dennis's Poultry Farm near Southfleet in Kent after receiving several direct hits in a bombing raid in July 1940. At the time, Mr Dennis was seen with tears in his eyes wheeling load after load of dead chickens to the incinerator and finishing off badly injured birds.

otherwise it had not been affected. This explanation is understandable because after so many years the Norfolk reed has settled down into a solid mass which it would be difficult to disturb, so completely has it been consolidated under the influence of rain and sun and wind.

So the Germans taught me to be thankful that I indulged in my fancy for Norfolk thatch. We probably owe our lives to it, as a roof of tiles or slate would almost certainly have been shattered by the explosions and would have fallen upon us, as it did in the case of the near-by cottages. When the war is over and reed can be transported from Norfolk and the craftsmen are available, I shall have any necessary repairs to the roof carried out, for the sake of appearances. In the meantime, the thatched roof is completely water-tight.

I am inclined to say, with a little grandchild who slept through a raid, now living in another part of the country: 'How annoyed Hitler would be if he knew how little we cared for his bombs.'

Livestock casualties were fewer than might have been expected – 560 were reported by the end of August 1940, including animals killed outright and those being treated for injuries from which they might recover. Farmers in the south-east, however, were particularly hard hit, and not slow to express a grievance. One wrote to *The Farmers Weekly* on 12th July 1940:

Sir, – During one night last month in an enemy air raid, I had 59 sheep killed and wounded. I reported the matter, and the Ministry of Food vans came and took away ten. Owing to delay, seven of these had to be condemned.

So far I have received for the 10 sheep £2 1s 6d. The country wants us to produce more food, yet I shall have to wait until after the war before I get the whole money for the 59 sheep. How can I replace my stock if no insurance is to be paid?

Of the 59 sheep, 26 were buried in the bomb-craters. Couldn't some of that meat have been saved and ground up for poultry or pig food? With meat and bone meal at £20 a ton, it seems to me to be downright waste to bury a ton of meat.

I need the money to restock my farm. Cannot anything be done to get payment before the war ends?

Usually, any livestock that was killed in air raids and was still fit for human consumption was bought by the Ministry of Food and paid for at casualty rates. Farmers were reminded that unless animals were bled and disembowelled immediately after being killed, the meat was not likely to be passed for human consumption. If necessary, owners could undertake the task themselves, but where possible they should without delay secure the services of a local butcher or divisional animal steward.

The reactions of animals to air raids were a matter of considerable dispute. The street horse, already trained to the noise of motor traffic, seemed little affected by the sound of high explosive bombs, perhaps regarding them as a sort of exaggerated backfire. Urban horses that retired to the land for lighter agricultural work at the age of 9 or 10 seemed to take the nonchalance with them. Younger horses were more wont to panic, but could soon become used to the sounds of war, like the bay gelding turned out into a very unhealthy area of Kent which, at the sound of a dogfight, simply galloped across the field and stood under the hedge until it was all over. Pigs, too, could be oblivious to the surrounding mayhem – one herd continued 'to snore sonorously' in a bombed slaughterhouse while the roof was blown to pieces around them. Cows, on the other hand, seemed to have reacted to stress by showing a diminished milk yield, and more than one farmer was able to persuade his local War Ag that a butter fat deficiency in his milk was due to the effects of an air raid.

In November 1940, the Under-Secretary for War, Sir Edward Grigg, re-emphasised the importance that the government attached to the Home Guard. Giving commissioned rank to Home Guard officers would enable them, if necessary, to take charge of regular troops. There was to be better equipment and training, and *esprit de corps* was to be nurtured so that, as the immediate danger of invasion receded, Home Guard units would feel that there was more to look forward to than routine training of uncertain worth.

Home Guards learning how to harass low-flying aircraft during training in northern England.

A further change for the better came during the winter of 1940 when Home Guard units which had been making do with nothing more by way of uniform than arm-bands, were issued with serge Army-issue battledress so that platoons assumed a more homogeneous and soldierly appearance.

The question of uniform had come up in a different context at Hampshire Quarter Sessions during the height of the invasion scare in June 1940. Counsel's opinion was sought as to the legal position of an L.D.V. volunteer who shot an enemy parachutist. The legality of the act was held to depend on how the enemy was clad – that is to say whether he was wearing his country's uniform, in which case it was proper to shoot him, or disguised as a civilian, in which case he should be detained as a spy and brought before the military authorities for interrogation. In Hertfordshire, William Petch received different advice. He could shoot any parachutist, however clothed, but he had first to ensure that he had donned his own denim uniform. So he rolled it up under his arm and took it to work with his rifle every day, just in case.

As the Home Guard began to get better weapons, the variety of different types of rifle caused perplexity, as they differed greatly in modernity and efficiency. Those, like the American Springfield .300 rifle, which had been packed away in heavy grease for years, needed hours of soaking in scalding water and thorough cleaning before they were usable. The British rifle of World War I – the Lee Enfield .303 – was more popular, and the modern shortened version of it was issued to some units by the end of 1940.

Platoons still looked forward to the day when they could lay hands on a Browning repeating rifle, a Thompson sub-machine gun or a Lewis or Vickers light machine-gun. When the guns arrived, instruction books were eagerly pored over until they eventually made sense, and the weapons were assembled, stripped down and then reassembled time after time until the operations were slick and professional. The winter was a time for lectures and drills, for learning how to use a Mills grenade and a whole miscellany of anti-personnel and anti-tank devices. As A.G. Street wrote,

Home Guard exercise in Scotland in the summer of 1941: an attack on a road block by the enemy, assisted by a fifth-columnist, who lies dead in the foreground.

When no outside lecturer was available, the ex-soldiers became amateur school masters for one hot smoky hour, and even drew curious diagrams on the blackboard to illustrate the lessons. Their methods were unorthodox, and their language often unprintable, but they got their points home.

The younger or more able members of a platoon might be sent out to a Sunday training camp, for instance to discover how to overcome problems with their weapons at least risk to themselves. Hand grenades were notoriously tricky, and incorrect use was likely to lead to mutilation or worse. They also showed an alarming tendency not to explode on impact, leaving the unfortunate platoon leader to make up his mind whether the grenade was a dud or not. Surprisingly, injuries do not seem to have been particularly numerous. This was in part due to the scarcity of ammunition, when not only bullets, shells and grenades were in short supply, but even blanks were hard to come by, and many exercises had to be completed to energetic shouts of 'bang bang' or the throwing of bags of sand at appropriate moments. Arthur Street commented:

One army trick that every civilian Home Guard soon learned from these exercises was the art of scrounging. The official issue of blanks, of thunder flashes, and all necessities for them was very small and often non-existent; so the good Guard officer and section leader supplemented it by devious means. Regulars were billeted in every house in the countryside, and the amount of useful stuff that their Home Guard war time hosts coaxed out of them is nobody's business.

William Petch was able to get rid of his American rifle, which did not work, by swapping it for a British rifle that did, the transaction being effected with a man who had just been called up into the Fleet Air Arm. The trick was undoubtedly not unique.

But even taking into account all the inadequacies and the local improvisation, the clothing, equipment and training of the Home Guard was a remarkable achievement, every bit as notable as the response by its one and a half million volunteers and their continued sacrifice of leisure and comfort during the winter months. Nevertheless the very rapidity with which the Home Guard had been organised brought inevitable divergences of view over its military status and tactics in

Home Guards learn to take advantage of natural cover when stalking. The Fieldcraft School of South Eastern Command, January 1942.

In a Home Guard demonstration in November 1942, a sniper emerges from cover. In his garb of sacking dyed green and brown, he is said not to be seen even at a few yards.

the field. One view was that the very strength of the service lay precisely in its local nature: the unit of tactics, as of personnel, should be the village. It was essentially a guerrilla force and could not successfully be adapted to the requirements of King's Regulations. Such misgivings were expressed by senior army officers, many of whom continued to deny that the Home Guard had any useful role to perform. There was also a certain amount of snobbery which affected the Home Guard in much the same way as it did the Women's Land Army. A War Office edict of 1941 which declared that Home Guard officers should travel third class on the railways made Major Jarvis almost apoplectic with rage:

I try *not* to think about it [the decision], as when one runs up against a cheap cheese paring policy of this description, combined with such

The Home Guard at Holy Island, off the coast of Northumberland, practise on the beach in June 1942. Nearly all of them are fishermen.

lack of realism, it is better not to disturb one's peace of mind in vain imaginings as to the mentality that conceived this amazing order.

The morale of the Home Guard had a big boost in 1941, when David McClean, a Scottish farm worker and member of a local Home Guard unit, had the distinction of capturing Rudolf Hess, Hitler's Deputy, at the end of his flight from Germany to Glasgow. Shortly after this, and giving the royal stamp of approval, came a summons from King George VI for the Home Guard to furnish the morning guard at Buckingham Palace.

By 1941, most people had become accustomed to the routine of wartime. Sometimes their laconic attitude towards Nazi bombs verged on the foolhardy. One farmer had eight delayed-action bombs on his fields. Six of them he left for the bomb disposal squad, but two were on land that he wanted to plough right away. So he simply dug them up himself, and loaded them on to his tractor trailer to get them out of the way. Another dealt with the two bomb craters and several unexploded bombs on his arable land by levelling the craters and ploughing in, or over, the dud bombs. Yet another farmer got a nasty surprise after an aerial dog fight when his shepherd invited him to his hut to show him a row of unexploded Messerschmitt cannon shells, which were said to explode if they touched so much as a hair. More cautious spirits, remembering the day and night air attacks of autumn 1940, when men in the fields were machine-gunned, urged farmers to let their hedges grow to provide cover.

At the beginning of 1942, the Ministry of Home Security withdrew the right of part-time civil defence workers to resign, a move that was resented by many as it deprived them of their liberty of action. The Home Guard was brought within the provisions for military conscription: any male civilian between 18 and 25 could now be directed to enroll in his local platoon for anything up to 48 hours a month. Until 16th February, men had the opportunity of resigning under the old terms of voluntary enlistment, and, with the waning of the invasion threat, some did, feeling that their efforts were better devoted to their full-time work which could itself be important in the war.

To a youth like Cyril Maddocks of Whitchurch in Shropshire, the Home Guard could be a big adventure: 'as a sixteen-year old I had a rifle and 60 rounds of ammunition in the wardrobe.' He could see, though, that 'not everyone enjoyed it.' The compulsion to join the Home Guard was resented by not a few farmers and labourers, and Maddocks recalled that in his Home Guard unit 'most of the men were farm labourers working very long hours and doing hard manual work, and to lose most of Sunday and sometimes two nights off per week was no small thing.'

The difficulty of reconciling farming with Home Guard duties led to a small but growing number of prosecutions for refusal to enroll or to attend parades. The 25-year-old son of a farmer from Abergavenny in Wales was fined £5 in December 1942 for refusing to join the Home Guard. The defendant said that he would rather go to prison than pay the fine, as he had no savings. He told the court that he worked from 7 a.m. to 10 p.m. every day for his father, who gave him only pocket money. Another farmer, Edward Wright of Bickleigh Farm at Milverton near Taunton in Somerset was fined the much larger sum of £50 with 3 guineas costs at Wiveliscombe Petty Sessions in March 1943 for failure to enrol. He pleaded that he worked every day from early morning to late at night and considered that his two younger brothers should be enrolled first. In a third case, Thomas Rees of Crossenny near Monmouth told the Appeals Commitee of Monmouth Quarter Sessions in April 1944 that he had failed to attend Home Guard parades because 'his usual working week averaged 80 hours: he often worked till 1 a.m. and had worked threshing machines until 11 p.m. by moonlight or artificial light.' He claimed that on the days in question farm work was 'a reasonable excuse' within the meaning of the Defence (Home Guard) Regulations. He was excused for non-attendance of one parade, but not for another two on which the conviction stood.

Home Guard commanders, who might be ex-army or retired colonial officers, often knew little about farming, and it was a common grievance among farm workers who were already working long hours that missing an attendance because of some unavoidable reason like having a cow calve could mean being ordered to make up for it on another night of the week.

Some concessions were made in September 1943. Men who worked more than a regular 60-hour week might apply for easement of their Home Guard duties, but the decision rested entirely with the local commander – an unsatisfactory situation. Farm workers who did fire-watching duties were to be exempt from watching outside the farm if they worked more than 60 hours a week unless exceptional circumstances made it imperative.

Conscientious objectors to Home Guard duty were rare, but one farmer at Preston in Lancashire, John Cookson, aged 29, stood firmly by his pacifist views. When directed to enrol in the Home Guard at Chipping in 1943, he returned the notice endorsed to the effect that he could not, as a Christian, comply with the order. Asked by Clitheroe Magistrates if he did not consider the production and distribution of milk was assisting the war effort he replied 'Farming is the job I do in peacetime.' The Chairman of the Bench, however, told the defendant that he had not the slightest sympathy with him: 'You must go to prison for 3 months and pay the costs.'

The Home Guard gathered up a motley collection of individuals ranging from schoolboys to hardened veterans of World War I. As Cyril Maddocks remembers, there were often few concessions made for the boy soldiers:

After one of our night exercises Bill Jones announced that he would certainly have been captured if he had not advanced backwards. After that he was known as Advance Backwards Jones. On another occasion, returning from manoeuvres, I stopped at the Bull and

Dog. It seems incredible now but I, in full battle dress and rifle, was considered too young to go in and Lieutenant Tom Jones brought me out a drink of orange.

Nevertheless there was at least one compensation: if he wore his Home Guard greatcoat, Cyril was allowed to get into pictures at forces prices.

During the course of 1942 and 1943, the Home Guard changed from being a largely static force, anchored to road blocks and observation posts, and acquired a more dynamic role suited to modern warfare. Many of the old sandbagged defences were pulled down, and units were equipped with spigot mortars, flame throwers and fougasses, as well as an assortment of bombs and sub-artillery. In open country, the riflemen and machine gunners of the old Home Guard would have been useless against armoured vehicles, but it was reckoned that a mobile squad, properly armed, might inflict quite a bit of damage on the enemy.

Accordingly, the Home Guard embarked on new exercises designed to convert it into a mobile defence force. These reached an apogee in 1944 when there was thought to be a risk that Germany might try to head off invasion with mass parachute drops into southern England. To leave regular troops free to continue with the build-up towards D-Day, the Home Guard was left to locate and deal with any intruders.

For their new training, the Home Guard sometimes received extraordinary manuals. Major Jarvis reported in *Country Life* in February 1944:

A Home Guard correspondent sent me a copy of a training circular which has been passed round in his area, and which consists of notes on jungle and river fighting. I should imagine that the pamphlet might be of considerable value to units which may be proceeding to the Far East shortly, but it is doubtful if a Home Guard unit located in an open down country will be able to apply any of the teachings about jungle clearance and mosquito precautions during its weekly parades. A most interesting paragraph about dealing with hostile river craft falls on somewhat barren ground, as the drawback to this area is that it is almost entirely waterless, and the biggest stream in the county holds nothing larger than 4oz trout and would float nothing of greater tonnage than a child's yacht.

For the two years before the Normandy landings on 6th June 1944, the countryside was filled with the sound of military activity and preparations for the offensive. New airfields for Bomber, Fighter and Coastal Commands came into operation, with more squadrons than ever before. Cyril Maddocks recalls:

Shropshire had many training airfields and the sky was full day and night if flying was at all possible. Every day you might see Ansons, Oxfords, Wellingtons, Lancasters, Spitfires, Mosquitos, Halifaxes, Stirlings or Hansa gliders. And then perhaps Mustangs, Liberators, Dakotas and Fortresses. I was always being told to get on with my work and not to look up at the aircraft.

Less prominent than the fighting commands of the RAF but growing at just as great a rate was Maintenance Command. *Illustrated* magazine described how 'wherever you go among the units you find "Maintenance" spread over great areas of countryside employing many thousands of people, a good half of them civilians.' Well-camouflaged and hidden away in rural areas were huge storage depots containing 'aircraft for Russia, trainers for Canada and America, spares for Libya, air supplied for Africa, India and catapult aircraft for the Merchant Service.' The reporter was impressed:

I saw a sample order come in from a bombing station during the morning. It was the wildest mixture of demands imaginable. 'One landing wheel for a Stirling X-type – four Browning .303s – one starboard mini-plane for Stirling – twenty pairs of WAAF's shoes of following sizes – one office table – five cases of flares – one bomb sight, type X – two stewpans – one half dozen of brandy (medical stores) – one power-driven gun turret with so-and-so mounting . . .' And that is all I can remember.

Apart from the land taken by the RAF for its air fields and storage depots, more was required by the army for battle training. During the war, approximately 600,000 acres of agricultural land was taken for defence purposes. Even though much of it was large tracts of unproductive moorland in Wales, Scotland and Yorkshire, considerable hardship was caused there to rural communities dependent on sheep farming. In Brecon and Radnorshire, some 79 farmers, most of whom spoke only Welsh, were dispossessed when 45,000 acres were commandeered in 1940. They were offered inadequate compensation, and many of them never returned to take possession of their farms after the war.

Sometimes the best agricultural land was taken, including 3,000 acres of growing corn in East Anglia in July 1942. An even larger area of rich pasture was commandeered in April 1943 in the East Riding of Yorkshire, affecting nearly 10,000 people and 50,000 head of livestock. In the House of Commons, the local M.P. Sir Herbert Williams asked: 'Do I understand that all battles take place on flat land?' 'No,' replied the War Secretary Sir James Grigg, 'but tank battles do not take place on mountain tops either.'

In Dorset, the tank range at Lulworth was extended to provide room for the Allied preparations for D-Day. The 225 villagers of Tynham and Worbarrow, which fell within the new boundaries,

146

were asked to evacuate their homes. They moved out just before Christmas 1943, leaving a notice pinned to the church door saying, 'Please treat our church and houses with care. We have given up our homes, where many of us have lived for generations, to help win the war to keep men free. We shall return one day and thank you for treating our village kindly.' But they were never allowed back: the valley was compulsorily purchased and sealed off in 1952, and even limited access was not restored until 1975.

'Defence vandalism' was a sore point with many a farmer. 'Is there any sense,' wrote one to *The Farmers Weekly* in August 1940, 'in driving tanks and lorries through crops of standing corn and over fences and fields containing cattle, allowing them to stray all over the district? Everybody knows that real military necessity comes before everything. Nevertheless there is a right and a wrong way to proceed.'

Solutions were not always easy to find. One farmer whose fields were used for summer evening walks by the troops from the neighbouring military camp was so incensed by his gates being left open, letting his cattle into the fields where he was growing oats, that he went to see the C.O. of the camp. After the troops received a lecture on the evils of leaving open farm gates, their behaviour changed dramatically. 'Now, if the beggars find a gate that is meant to be open, they shut that, too! I turn my cows out into a paddock after milking and leave the gate open for 'em to go out into the meadows. Came home t'other evening and heard 'em bellowing like hell. The troops had shut 'em in the paddock!'

A farmer's wife from Barton-under-Needwood in Staffordshire, Mrs Hugh Taylor, remembers another incident:

One evening a huge Wellington bomber landed in our freshly sown field of wheat. They had had to make a forced landing. We soon found that we were entertaining six tall handsome airmen . . . After the young men had recovered from their shock, the pilot asked if he might telephone his Commanding Officer. My husband took him to the office and heard him say 'Yes sir, yes sir.' Silence, and then 'No sir.' The vital question had been, 'Did you switch over to the other tank,' and the answer had to be 'No sir, I forgot.' . . . A day or two later the bomber was towed away across the fields leaving a very rough patch in the cornfield and a large gap in the thorn hedge.

Apart from commandeering land to use in training for the duration of the war, the army also turned up for exercises in extensive areas populated by civilians. One of the largest was code-named Spartan, and *Illustrated* magazine described it in May 1943:

For nearly a month the towns and villages and countryside of Southern and Eastern England, and the sky above have been a battleground for hundreds of thousands of men.

Cottagers have been awakened in the night by the vast processions of sombre armoured shapes travelling without lights in the blackout.

Farmers found silent, armed men in the barns.

The housewife's daily shopping round has been held up by the passage of endless lines of vehicles and marching men. And millions of other members of the public have suffered a certain amount of personal inconvenience, irritation and loss. All this has led to wild rumours and wilder surmise . . .

All troops taking part were ordered to consider themselves in an administrative desert as far as supplies were concerned. No officer or man of all the huge number engaged was allowed to enter a shop or restaurant to buy food.

The armies had to be absolutely self-sufficient and utilise none of the normal civilian services. Most of the troops slept rough and lived on 'iron rations.' In brief, they had to live and fight precisely as if they were engaged in actual enemy territory where civilian services were non-existent or at a minimum.

The primary object of 'Spartan' was to practise big advances from bridgeheads into a closely built-up countryside with an abundance of natural obstacles like rivers, streams, hills and woods, in the face of a determined enemy who would take every advantage of those obstacles.

Unlike military exercises of the past on manoeuvre grounds like Salisbury Plain, real towns and villages had to be attacked or defended. Also it was a try-out under active service conditions of a new system of control of air forces operating with the army . . .

The general scheme of 'Spartan' was as follows. A Southern army, under Lieut-General McNaughton, comprising Canadian and British divisions and armoured units, including the Guards Armoured Division, 'landed' on the South Coast, established bridgeheads and struck north to the Eastland border.

This was a line running roughly round southern London, curving north-west to the south of Aylesbury, skirting Banbury and turning south-west again along the border of Worcestershire to the Bristol Channel.

Westland, the area west of Worcester, Birmingham, Stafford was 'neutral' territory not to be touched by either side during the course of the manoeuvres. The Eastland Army (the 'German Army') under the command of Lieut-General Gammell, was composed mainly of British units. When the battle began, the Southern Army 'on paper' made big commando-led raids on the East Coast and established bridgeheads to divert still more of his strength.

General McNaughton's objective was Eastland's 'capital' of Huntingdon. If General Gammell could prevent the taking of his 'capital' for one week from zero hour, then he was reinforced and so would have a 'paper' victory. As a matter of fact, he succeeded in doing so.

Losses or victories in a mimic war may seem a futile thing to refer to in the midst of an actual war. But the main reasons for Gammell's success formed probably the most valuable part of 'Spartan'.

He struck south across his border with great speed and across the line of the Thames and Kennet and proceeded to lay minefields in the path of the Southern advance and make demolitions on a colossal scale.

He blew up every bridge as he retired north again across the rivers.

I was with the Southern Army during its advance and watched prodigious feats of bridge-building carried out against time and under 'fire' – work which certainly could not be performed under ordinary training conditions.

Near Reading, for instance, a bridge able to carry heavy armoured vehicles was thrown across in a few hours by men who had been working on other bridge building for over thirty hours without a break.

Military umpires, of whom there were thousands engaged in the exercise, saw to it that the new bridge was completed and able to carry traffic before the original 'demolished' bridge was opened again for the held up Southern forces.

They ruled rigidly on the number of casualties sustained in aircraft attacks. One bridging company sustained 60 per cent 'casualties', which naturally impeded progress on that particular bridge. All casualties had to go back through the normal channels as in actual war. The sappers went on ahead of the forces clearing 'minefields.' And though these of course were merely dummies, represented by bricks and the like, all had to be searched for and cleared as if they

American paratroops training in the English countryside in September 1942.

were real mines.

Sometimes it seemed a game, but it was played in deadly earnest, under the gaze of countless people going about their ordinary business. It was a vital preparation for the grim actuality of war . . .

There was, of course, much damage to private property, some of it grievous, but almost all of it unavoidable.

To the householder who waked to find his favourite flower bed draped round his chimney pots by the tracks of a deploying tank, I can only pass on a remark I heard from an old gentleman in a Hampshire lane.

A lovely eighteenth-century wall and wrought iron gates to his house had been smashed by a tank careening in the blackout as it was travelling into action.

'Oh, well,' he said, 'it might have been done by a German bomb, and I'm *sure* a German tank would have made a much bigger mess of it.'

In the same way, every citizen who has suffered loss in this manner should consider it his private contribution to the success of 'Exercise Spartan.' Some day we will know that 'Spartan' hammered out the formula for our victory on the Continent. And that should be a sufficient compensation.

As the day of the cross-channel assault drew nearer, it seemed that much of rural England was being turned into a vast army camp. In November 1943, some 35 square miles of Devon were taken over; 3,000 people were evacuated from the villages and 200 farmers were dispossessed. The south-west was a key area because troops needed to be trained in areas as similar as possible to those where they would land in northern Europe, and so Devon stood in for Normandy. The rehearsals for landing in France clearly required the utmost secrecy, and civilians had to be kept out of the way.

The requisitioning of land reached its peak in the early months of 1944. Members of the British First Airborne Division, who were to

American 4,000 lb bombs for Flying Fortresses being stored in a supply depot in February 1944.

be the heroes of Arnhem, trained in the Yorkshire Wolds, and there seemed to be Americans everywhere else. Indeed, just before D-Day, over 3 million acres of England, Wales and Northern Ireland, one thirteenth of the total land area, had to be set aside temporarily for the training of American forces.

With such a build-up of troops and materials, the preparations could not be kept entirely from public knowledge. A motorist driving through Savernake Forest in Wiltshire was astounded to see tank after tank lined up in apparently unending numbers. A troop of boy scouts camping on the fringes of Dartmoor came across hundreds of lorries marshalled for shipment overseas. Near Branston in Devon, holidaymakers were turned away from the caves, which were being used as an enormous artillery store. Throughout May and the first days of June 1944, convoys of military vehicles could be seen on near-deserted roads, gradually converging on the embarkation ports. The Winchester By-Pass, which had been completed just before the outbreak of war, was not open to civilian traffic, as it was being used to park military transport and armoured vehicles in readiness for moving them to Southampton for Operation Overlord itself.

The D-Day offensive of 6th June 1944 left the countryside seeming almost abnormally quiet with most of the troops gone. But it was only a week before the quiet was shattered by the first flying bombs, which hit Kent and London on 13th June. In the following 80 days some 2,400 bombs fell in the countryside – a hundred more than London suffered. Although they were widely distributed, there was a heavy concentration in the corridor between Dover and the Romney Marsh, stretching up between Maidstone and Tunbridge Wells to London. In addition to the bombs came a rain of ack-ack shells, fighter plane bullets and cannon shells fired in an effort to bring down the bombs before they reached the capital. Alan Ramsay visited Kent on 8th August to report for *The Farmer & Stock-breeder*:

Once again the fields of southern England are the graveyards of German air weapons. Four years ago I visited this part of the countryside and saw how food producers were defying the air might of the Luftwaffe. To-day the story is being repeated although the enemy's tactics are changed. Now it is the flying bomb that falls victim to shell, fighter-plane and balloon barrage.

Last week-end I stood on a hillside overlooking one of those typical strips of S. England which under different circumstances would have been alive with motorists. The only noise was the unmistakable roar of an approaching bomb on its way to London. But it never got there. A Spitfire swooped, a gun rattled, the bomb exploded and that was that. A common sight in this part of the country; the complete answer to the latest phase of indiscriminate bombing.

Unfortunately, however, the answer is not always so effective. Sometimes the bird is only winged: there is a mad and uncertain swoop to earth and a pillar of foul-smelling smoke marks the scene of destruction. It may be in a field of ripening wheat, it may be beside a group of cows, it may be on a farm-house or its adjacent buildings. That is just the luck of war.

It is this uncertainty which makes the life of the S. England food producer a trifle hectic these days, not so hectic that he or she neglects the essential jobs of gathering in the harvest of the field or the orchards but just enough to make the strain felt. Sleeping at nights with one eye open – or should we say with one ear alert – is not the best preparation for a hard day's work.

When the full story of this area comes to be told we shall know just how much damage was done to the buildings and how many livestock met an untimely end. These things are not inconsiderable. But if the visitor in peacetime misses something attractive from the landscape he will know that in its place there is something more enduring than bricks and mortar, the spirit of a people who were not to be terrified as the enemy had planned.

This spirit is soon caught by those who come into the holiday camps. There was an instance of this the other night when a party arrived on its first day. About midnight a flying bomb was caught in a near-by balloon cable. The balloon was set on fire – an awe-inspiring sight in itself – and the bomb landed some hundred yards away, bringing down many of the tents and neatly removing the roof of the kitchen.

In charge of the camp was a retired naval officer who was not to be unduly disturbed by such trifles. Having made certain that no-one was injured, he set about having the tents replaced and finished up with a reminder to the visitors that the coaches would be calling at 8.15 to take them to work. No-one missed the coach.

Kent was not the only county affected. B. Green of Farnham in Surrey remembers that as an eleven-year-old:

I was walking my dog when I saw a V-1 rocket coming towards me, then it stopped and dived into a farmyard half a mile in front. I ran there, the dog ran in front. The farmer had just brought the cattle to the yard and it landed in the middle. It flattened everything, sheds, haystacks, walls, house. I walked through a mountain of chopped up cattle and debris. The family was underneath but I didn't know. I walked away again before anyone came. Nobody knew I had been there. I think one of the family survived.

In July, Land Girls in the southern counties were again issued with steel helmets as a protection against flying bombs, and despite the evident danger carried on their work. One unwelcome interruption was hoards of sightseers who arrived daily and were reported in *The Farmer & Stock-breeder* as doing 'serious damage to the crops in their eagerness to see the effects of flying bombs and to collect souvenirs.' The Government later warned that such behaviour was against the law and that offenders risked a heavy fine if they were caught.

The quiet heroism of country people was recognised in the award of medals and decorations. A Kentish farmer, Gilbert Mitchell, and his wife were awarded the George Medal and British Empire Medal respectively for their 'sustained bravery and devotion to duty, in the face of enemy bombing, shelling and machine-gun fire.' The B.E.M. was also awarded to Grace Harrison, the Land Girl who assisted them at Reach Farm near Dover, which was at the nearest point to the Continent and was scarred with filled-in shell holes and had the most vulnerable farm buildings in the country. This was in May 1942, and Mr Mitchell, who farmed 120 acres, was to take charge of six more farms totalling about 2,700 acres on behalf of the Kent War Ag. Other country people received awards and citations for attempting to rescue aircrew from crashed planes. Perhaps more amazing was the achievement of three farm labourers in saving their West Country village from evacuation. E. Fowler, who was a member of the Home Guard, and two eighteen-year-olds, R. Russell and J. Eastment, succeeded in digging out a large bomb in February 1941 when no bomb disposal squad was available. There were instances, too, when airmen gave their lives to save a village. Thus, in May 1942, Pilot Officer Richard Pryce Hughes was killed when deliberately steering his damaged plane clear of a Hampshire village. He had been manager of his father's *estancia* in Argentina, where he kept a herd of shorthorns, and had joined the Royal Canadian Air Force at the outbreak of war.

The doodlebug menace slowly abated in the Autumn of 1944. The success of the Allied Armies on the other side of the English Channel allowed restrictions gradually to be lifted and by mid-September coastal towns from the Wash to Bournemouth were once more open to the public. Home Guard drills ceased to be compulsory and men were no longer drafted into the service. Large numbers of Civil Defence workers went part-time and, although the south of England was not yet exempt, most country fire guard duties came to an end. But best of all for people's spirits was the lifting of the black-out. As *The Field* commented ecstatically:

Five years of war more or less in the front line have weighed heavily on the civilian population, but nothing has weighed so heavily, caused so much irritation or so much depression as the black-out. Furthermore, although the attacks of the Luftwaffe – and some of them were very heavy – were directly mainly at the civilian population, the civilian population suffered heavier casualities through the black-out than through the bombing. There could have been no greater tonic.

On 3rd December 1944 came the final stand-down parade of the Home Guard before the King in London's Hyde Park. There were those who regretted the decision of the War Office, seeing it as premature – others even itched for action in France. But for most country people the end of Home Guard duties came as a relief and allowed them to return to their proper business. They had cause for pride in their war service, and Major Jarvis aptly summed up their feelings in *Country Life*:

And now we middle-aged and elderly men have turned over a page in our lives' histories, which we did not expect, and which is a very much fuller and more closely-written page than we imagined it would be when we first started it. It is on the whole a pleasant and comforting page to look back at as, among other assets, we have got to know intimately and to appreciate at their real worth so many men who, in other circumstances, would have been mere business and shopping contacts. Mr. Jones is no longer the shop assistant who sold us hammers, chisels and lawn-mowers but be-medalled Sergeant Jones, who never missed a parade and who could make sections jump to it. Mr. Brown, the gunsmith, who in the past supplied us with cartridges, is the mechanical expert, who, in addition to drills, worked all hours of the night repairing and cleaning old weapons; and Mr. Smith, the cinema manager, is our signalling officer, and, judging by the efficiency of his detachment, it is pity perhaps that he left the Army in 1918 for his present calling, which a lesser man might manage. There is hardly an able-bodied man in the town and on the surrounding farms who we do not know – and respect; and, if this is reciprocated, it may count for something in the difficult years to come.

A few more months of war remained. Sadly, there were still to be civilian victims. On 9th March 1945 a lone German aircraft, after machine-gunning a farmstead and a number of cottages in a north-eastern village, crashed on the farmhouse, killing the farmer, Richard Moll, his wife Helen, and her daughter-in-law, Violet. The son, Fred Moll, with his three-year old son Edgar in one hand, tried to force his way through the flames and debris, beating out the fire with his free hand. He succeeded, but his wife and parents died in hospital of their injuries. The indomitable spirit of the countryside at war was epitomised in a column published by Arthur Street in *The Farmers Weekly* on 6th November 1942, at a time when the outcome of the conflict was by no means certain:

The other day I found myself in a typical downland village. For security reasons I cannot give its rightful name but will call it Sedgebury Wallop. The sun was shining, the time was 3 p.m., and I was watching an old dairyman and his little grandson driving some cows along the lane for the afternoon milking.

Suddenly the local air raid siren began to scream its warning of approach of enemy aircraft.

'Hitler's whistle, grandad, Hitler's whistle' shrilled the child, and he whacked Buttercup with his stick to make that patient beast hurry up.

'Thee let she bide,' said the ancient, 'an' let un blow. Thease cows maun be milked whatever.'

The siren gave its last wail, as two local Air Raid Wardens in steel helmets and Sunday blue suits cycled hurriedly down the lane to their posts.

Apart from this one sign of war the English scene remained unaltered. The sun still shone brightly. The cows pad-padded slowly up the lane. Parents and children continued their Sunday walk towards the woods. The sparrows went on twittering in the thatch, and the village still blinked cosily in the sunlight, its houses and cottages clustering around the church and the pub as from time immemorial.

Suddenly the local ack-ack gave tongue, and then came four or five ominous crumps evidently not too far away, for a loose glass in one of my car doors shivered audibly in response. But in spite of this Sedgebury Wallop, its people, and its surroundings just carried on undisturbed.

It was a short alert, for by the time the first spurt of milk tinkled pleasantly into the pail between the old man's knees, the all-clear sounded. And once again the little boy piped up that it was 'Hitler's whistle, grandad, Hitler's whistle.'

And as I listened to the siren a most comforting thought came to me. 'These things,' I muttered, 'Sedgebury Wallop, its cows, its thatch, its church, its inn, its fields and crops, its men, women and children, all the English scene – these things will remain and thrive when Hitler's whistle is but a memory.'

Chapter 5
SOCIAL EFFECTS OF THE WAR

There was a feeling among wartime city dwellers that country people had all the luck, being better fed and spared the ordeal of the blitz. A woman from the London suburb of Chingford in Essex who worked in a munitions factory and was forced to move to Pangbourne in Berkshire on doctor's orders in 1944 was most indignant that the villagers she met should 'make such a big thing about the one bomb or so' that dropped on nearby Reading – 'they didn't really know there was a war on'.

Country people, on the other hand, complained that no-one in the cities appreciated how much back-breaking work went into the rural war effort. Indeed, it was not too surprising that the farm workers who laboured from dawn to dusk 7 days a week should take umbrage at people from the towns being able to find time to come out for a relaxing country stroll.

Away from the south coast, the amount of bomb destruction in the countryside was certainly small. Some market towns and villages did suffer, but the loss of human life was negligible compared to that in the capital and in Coventry, Merseyside, Plymouth and Birmingham. In the area of the Thames Valley around Reading, for example, the most shocking spectacle of the war was not the occasional hit on the town but the ghastly illumination of the night sky in the east as London burned during the Blitz.

Further afield, even the sighting of an enemy plane could be unusual enough to be worthy of lengthy discussion at the local pub. The notion that one day a victorious Wehrmacht might march through the winding streets of a Cornish or Cumbrian village or intrude on

The Queen chats to two volunteer workers on a visit to a Ministry of Agriculture Volunteer Camp in the Home Counties.

At Barnwell Manor Home Farm on his estate, the Duke of Gloucester chats with a farmworker while helping with the harvest.

the peace of a Scottish glen seemed almost inconceivable. Just below the surface, though, was the feeling that this war was somehow different.

In the past, countrymen had gone off to fight, content in the knowledge that they had left their women and children safe at home – as one commentator put it, 'the children would almost certainly grow up to take our places: our eldest son and his family live in the old stead cottage our fathers made, which has been mended and improved, generation after generation.' But now 'everyone, no matter who they are or where they live, has this strange uncertainty about the future.' The awareness of the common danger, of all being in the same boat, went a long way towards overcoming petty rivalries between the classes or between town and country. In every possible way, each individual was reminded that he or she had a personal contribution to make to the war effort, a unique part to play in achieving final victory. One of the most potent symbols of national unity was provided by the Royal Family. The King and Queen remained steadfastly in Buckingham Palace during the worst of the bombing, but maintained an active interest in every type of war work. Country dwellers were pleased to hear that the King was 'an arable farmer', having consented to the ploughing up of 300 acres of the royal farm at Windsor and 1,000 acres of Windsor Great Park. Royal visits to country areas and volunteer labour camps drew attention to the importance of farming. One such visit took place in the summer of 1944, when their Majesties saw reclamation work being carried out at Maidenhead Thicket in Berkshire. After watching the patches of scrub being demolished by a Prairie-Buster plough, the royal couple took tea with the volunteers – townspeople who had offered seven days' service in the camp.

Even the Princesses Elizabeth and Margaret were enlisted to help, at first by gardening at their country refuge and by knitting for the forces. A correspondent in of *The Farmer & Stock-breeder* commented unkindly of the elder princess that, although helpful to her younger sister, 'she could not as yet successfully turn the heel of a sock alone and is dependent on her nurse, Mrs Knight, for some guidance and instruction.' That, however, was in 1940. By 1943, with such humble tasks behind them, the princesses had graduated to assisting with the harvest at Sandringham.

One of the more agreeable features of wartime life was the way in which whole communities would throw themselves into a campaign for some common cause. One such was organised by the National Savings Committee to convert peace-time savings into a massive public war fund. In 1939 there were some 42,000 savings groups in the entire country, but by the summer of 1943 the number had topped 300,000, of which just under half were organised in rural districts. The big campaigns such as War Weapons Week, Warships Week and Wings for Victory Week provided the chance for a show of local pageantry – colourful relief from the work a day monotony of wartime – as well as raising a large amount of money. Some villages made enormous efforts – Weston Turville in Buckinghamshire, with a population of about a thousand, raised £14 a head for the Wings for Victory Week, while E.M. Delafield reported that her

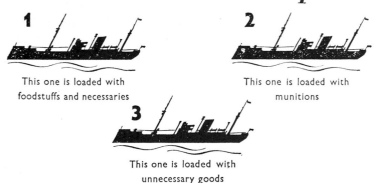

HINTS ON WAR-TIME SPENDING AND SAVING

Here are three ships

1 This one is loaded with foodstuffs and necessaries

2 This one is loaded with munitions

3 This one is loaded with unnecessary goods

By limiting your purchases of the goods con ained in Ship No. 3, you leave more cargo space for the goods we need to win the war. Spend carefully then—buy what you must—but avoid spending on unnecessary things, particularly goods which come from abroad.

Result: (1) *You increase the shipping available for essentials.*

(2) *You have more money to invest in National Savings Certificates and the New Defence Bonds.*

A five-year-old from Ullingswick in Herefordshire gives her pet lamb to the country Red Cross sale in August 1941. It realises over £30 for the Red Cross Agricultural Fund.

Devon parish of 700 souls, which did 'not include a single large estate or wealthy householder', raised £5,000 for War Weapons Week.

Another opportunity to raise money was the Red Cross Agriculture Fund, which was inaugurated by the Lord Mayor of London in May 1940 and had exceeded £5 million by the end of the war, some of it as the result of great money-making flair in some unexpected quarters. In September 1940, farmers at Uttoxeter in Staffordshire raised £10 by auctioning a leaflet dropped by a German plane, while in 1943 the North Armagh Hunt Club realised £17 10s from the sale of two bananas, a lemon and an onion, and the Lostwithiel District Allotments Association sent £5 raised by the sale of a freak potato

Children at the village school at Blean near Canterbury spend their summer holidays in 1941 helping with the school's War Savings campaign.

grown in the form of a Cornish cross. Other schemes run by the Fund included the weekly collection of Rural Pennies, the holding of Victory Garden Shows, and auction sales of prize or unusual livestock. Vicky, a V-marked Ayrshire heifer, toured country markets during the summer of 1943 to collect over £13,000 in contributions. The money made from these enterprises was spent on prisoner-of-war parcels, medical supplies, mobile canteens for blitzed areas and on special projects such as aid to Russia.

Other villages chose to send gifts directly to the Comforts Depots of the Navy, Army and Air Force. The tiny hamlet of Thrupp in Oxfordshire co-operated in an enormous knitting bee for the first Christmas of the war, amassing a vast collection of woollen scarves, socks, balaclavas, mittens and pullovers. Another huge parcel was sent by the Women's Working Party of Old Newton in Suffolk, yet another came from the Women's Land Army in Kent, and others came from every corner of the country.

Other villages or towns took another tack by setting up a Buy a Spitfire Club or by adopting a British ship or regiment. Thus, the country town of Amersham in Buckinghamshire adopted the submarine *Unbroken* during Navy Week 1943. In October of that year, Lieutenant Bevis Andrew, the commanding officer, together with the crew, spent a weekend in the town being fêted by the inhabitants. The climax of the festivities was a dinner given by the town council, above which hung the flag of the *Unbroken* – a Jolly Roger. The coxswain explained that the *Unbroken* had already sunk four enemy ships in its four patrols in the Mediterranean, which accounted for the bars on the flag; the daggers were for 'special duty', and the stars were for gunnery action in blowing up a train in Sicily.

These feats of arms may have seemed far removed from the routine of country life, but there was hardly a field of human endeavour on which the war did not have some impact. Even the most somnolent of rural institutions was roused from its torpor by new and harsh realities. As Colin Harris reported of one West Country church, 'the Rector now talks of everyday things – how we are to be brave when we are wakened up at night by enemy planes, to be patient with rations etc.' The sermons were listened to with rapt attention by smaller congregations than before, made up of women and older people who had gathered to pray for their husbands and sons, and to hear their names spoken one by one in the Intercession.

Policing was no longer the sole prerogative of the rural constabulary, whose traditional activities were supplemented by those of the Specials and the A.R.P., while men of the professional force were mobilised. A farmer's daughter from Haddenham in Cambridgeshire recalls:

At the outbreak of war, the local policeman, Sergeant Lees, who was on the reserve list, was called up. Sergeant Lees was a likable and pleasant man, he married a teacher from the village school and was happily settled in the Police House. Only a short while after he was called up – just a few weeks – the sad news was received of his death on active service. He was one of the first casualties. The former village policeman, an elderly retired constable, took over the duties until the end of the war.

Young or inexperienced new guardians of the law were likely to be met with resentment by villagers. Colin Harris commented:

The Specials are very grand with dark blue coats, rubber boots, a tin hat with letters in white paint and lots of power to keep us in order. They are enjoying their power, often the first they have had in their lives.

Not everyone, though, was overawed by the Specials or by the ARP. E.M. Delafield reported that a woman warden who had knocked up a householder to tell him 'There's an incendiary bomb in your house', received the curt rejoinder, 'And is that any business of yours?' She also had a friend who overheard her evacuee from Bethnal Green extemporising in the bathroom:

> Under the spreading chestnut tree
> Stands the bloody A.R.P.

Even the Town Crier, the oldest official in Miss Delafield's Devon village, was involved in A.R.P. duties when a number of enemy aircraft were sighted on a cold February morning in 1941 and the siren

Clement Davies, MP for Montgomeryshire, at Welshpool Smithfield during War Weapons Week in March 1941, when Montgomeryshire raised £638,000, against a target of only £250,000.

on the church tower had frozen solid. In his caped coat and three-cornered hat, ringing his bell, he groped his way up the slippery, blacked-out High Street crying 'Oyez, oyez, oyez! An alarm has been sounded; let all take cover.'

His was not the only rural calling to come into its own during the war. Ironically there was renewed demand for products of the village industries which had fallen sadly into decline. Thus, the loss of continental supplies of charcoal for use in steel production created an urgent need for the home-grown product. The Ministry of Supply responded by setting up charcoal plants in their traditional locations, and some firms were soon operating batteries of about 40 kilns. In spite of some rather primitive technology, home production was making up for the loss of charcoal imports by the autumn of 1940.

Other woodland industries also received a boost. Before the war, local craftsmen had been unable to compete with the mass-production methods used in Europe to make barrel hoops, and all the hoops used by British coopers were brought in from Holland, Belgium or south-west France. In Backbarrow, Newby Bridge and Furness in the Lake District, the industry had been defunct for so long that some of those who were called upon to rediscover their art were in their seventies and eighties. The half-forgotten skills of the Somerset willow industry were revived to provide urgently needed baskets for shell cases and containers for Red Cross field surgical equipment. As German clothes pegs with metal springs became unobtainable, New Forest gypsies began to make more of their traditional wooden pegs, and in Berkshire gypsies and other wooden-skewer-makers were turning spindle trees to their former use – with or without the permission of the landowner. In the Chilterns, the makers of tent-pegs were reported to be doing a brisk trade with the forces, and in Dorset and Cornwall home net-makers helped meet the greater demand for allotment nets as the factories had mainly gone over to making nets for military camouflage. The Dig for Victory campaign also benefited the potters whose products were needed to hold the greatly increased number of seedlings being raised for kitchen gardens. As sole leather for shoes became scarcer and more expensive, the clog makers in southern England and Wales returned to business. Three factors – the new reliance on shanks's pony that was encouraged by petrol rationing, the black-out and appeals from military hospitals – continued to help bring war work to the rural grower and manufacturer of walking sticks, whose craft was virtually moribund.

The return of the agricultural horse, partial although it was, inspired the revival of a whole range of crafts that supplied the needs of horse husbandry. In many villages, the forge had already closed down and the departure of the blacksmith had been accompanied

Charcoal burners in the Forest of Dean at Flaxley, Gloucestershire, in 1940.

160

Land Girls working in April 1940 at a new charcoal-producing plant set up in woodlands at Leckwith, near Cardiff. Apart from its industrial uses, charcoal had a new, wartime function as the filter in gas-masks.

by that of the saddler's shop and the many wainwrights and wheel-wrights, who used to make the farm carts and wagons, the wooden harrows, wooden plough frames and so on. In the autumn of 1940, these now essential craftsmen joined agricultural workers on the Schedule of Reserve Occupations so that they no longer had to join up, but there was still an acute lack of young people taking up these trades. *The Farmers Weekly* found that the two men employed by the 70-year-old harness maker in a small market town were both over 80. The elder referred to his junior as 'the boy'. A wheelwright, whose right-hand man, a lad of 33, had gone off to the army, had a yard full to overflowing with wagons and machinery awaiting attention, and more were being brought up the lane all the time.

Among the schemes introduced to deal with the shortage of rural craftsmen was the establishment in Herefordshire, Worcestershire and Gloucestershire of special schools for training young men as smiths. The schools enjoyed only limited success: a few of their students became technically proficient and started in business, but the continued trend towards mechanisation after the war, and the reappearance of manufactured imports, meant that the revival of rural industries was short-lived. Nevertheless, older men brought out of retirement welcomed the chance to be useful again and found themselves rejuvenated by their return to jobs that before the war had seemed old-fashioned.

Much of the burden of war in the countryside fell on the women, who took on many of the men's jobs. They worked in garages, de-livered goods, became postwomen and telephonists, and ran various local services, as well as doing their duty as wardens or fire watchers. The wife of the squire, rector or doctor was often an indispensable organiser. A Cambridgeshire diarist remembered one such lady:

Early on a very enthusiastic branch of the Red Cross was formed and run by Doctor and Mrs Fairweather who organised classes for members. The Lodge, Doctor Fairweather's home, was the head-quarters. In fact, the Lodge became the busiest house in Haddenham. Not only was it the First Aid Post, but the business of organising homes for evacuees was done there, with all the problems included in that undertaking. Mrs Fairweather was tireless and hardworking; it was amazing the amount of work and organising she did. One day she said to me 'You know I've got into a dreadful state, if I sit down

and do nothing I get such a guilty feeling.' Her house was chock-a-block full of blankets, gas masks, first-aid equipment, stretchers and clothing for evacuees.

At the age of 75, Bob Parris, a shepherd since he was nine, still, in April 1940, looking after a flock of 230 sheep at Crondall in Hampshire.

Women's organisations such as the Women's Institute, the Women's Voluntary Service and Church Guild assumed a new importance and were soon mounting their own special war effort. The W.I., for instance, initiated a great fruit-preserving drive to help maintain a healthy diet, using sugar made available by the Ministry of Food. The members either gave up their time to go to the local centre to help with the canning, bottling and jam-making or took a proportion of the sugar home with them to make preserves and sell them through the Institute. In the larger towns and villages, immense quantities of fruit were processed. A thousand new centres were set up at the beginning of the harvest season in 1940 and each received 20 to 25 cwt of sugar – Dorking in Surrey applied for as much as 3 tons. Even the smallest villages tried to do their bit, sometimes under adverse conditions. One, in East Kent, was next to an aerodrome, and was bombed so heavily that many of the houses were flattened and a good part of the population had to be evacuated. Membership of the W.I., which had stood at 108 before the war, fell to five, but the five still owned a canning machine. In 1940, in the midst of shelling and bombing, they managed to can 700 cwt of fruit, made 700 cwt of jam and filled 100 bottles of fruit. By the end of the war, some villages had produced, almost literally, mountains of jam. Rosedale, an isolated village on the North Yorkshire Moors, produced over 3½ tons of jam in a village reading room with no electricity, gas or water. All the cooking had to be done on an oil stove and the pails of water were brought on foot from a quarter of a mile away.

The W.V.S. was an early product of the war effort. It was formed in the spring of 1938 by the Dowager Marchioness of Reading on the initiative of the Home Secretary of the time, Sir Samuel Hoare, because there was no existing women's organisation that was suitable for recruiting women into the A.R.P. Its actual function was much wider, including all manner of voluntary support services. Broadly speaking, it saved the day in situations where official channels would have been too slow or inflexible to cope. Being thoroughly decentralised, it was well equipped to deal quickly with local problems as they arose. Thus, over the first weekend of the war, the Warwickshire W.V.S. responded to a shortage of mattresses for the floods of evacuees arriving in the countryside by making 1,000 mattress covers and stuffing them with straw. In *Women in Green*, Charles Graves recounts how at Menai Bridge in North Wales, the W.V.S. Village Representative walked ten miles to find a priest to comfort a small Roman Catholic boy who had broken his leg and felt convinced that this was a punishment for eating meat on a Friday.

The W.V.S. organised canteens for the services and the Merchant Navy, and mobile canteens for civil defence workers, at first improvising with whatever vehicles could be found. Charles Graves describes one such canteen based at Spalding in Lincolnshire:

. . . every day, rain or shine, a member of the W.V.S. set out from her home in East Anglia on a tour of Britain's bleakest marshes to cheer the isolated troops, who, in gratitude, called her 'The Florence Nightingale of the Marshes'. Through dense fogs and in the blackout she drove her camouflaged van fifty miles a day for six days a week. Half of it was fitted up as a canteen for selling tea and cakes. The other half was equipped as a shop in which she sold everything from hair oil to birthday cards for sweethearts. In the first fourteen weeks, the van travelled over four thousand miles, during which period twenty thousand cups of tea and thirty-seven thousand cakes were sold.

The W.V.S. was active, too, in organising salvage campaigns and actively promoted them with such snippets of information as: 'if every household threw into the dustbin a scrap of paper the size of a bus ticket each day, the loss to the country [would equal] one hundred and twenty million wads for small arms ammunition.' The County Herb Committees, organised by the W.I. with the co-operation of the W.V.S., collected and dried medicinal herbs from the countryside. By 1943, herb imports were down to half their pre-war level. The gathering of rose-hips from the hedgerows also happened under the aegis of the women's organisations. The manufacturers who made the hips into a vitamin-rich syrup for distribution to mothers and babies paid threepence a pound, and the harvest brought in its wake a mass of accounting and packing work. An appeal for horse chestnuts for pharmaceutical use produced such a response that W.V.S. offices nearly ground to a halt – sufficient supplies to last for the rest of the war arrived in a few weeks.

The National Federation of Women's Institutes also encouraged vegetable gardening by buying seed collections from seedsmen at bargain prices and distributing thousands of packets of onion, carrot, perpetual spinach and arctic lettuce seeds to its local centres. The arrangement worked well, but the N.F.W.I. contribution to the Dig for Victory campaign ran into ministerial red tape in the summer of 1940 with a plan for mobile gangs of Land Girls to cultivate abandoned gardens. The Ministry of Agriculture pointed out that there might be legal objections from owners who disapproved of their gardens being trampled upon, dug up and planted. This irritated Mary Day of *The Farmers Weekly*, who wrote that 'This government has shown already that it can straighten out legal muddles overnight when it has a mind to, or what else does the State ownership of property amount to? And as for strangers in the gardens – presently, I would rather think of Land Girls plodding their way over mine than have the Nazi army planting their boots on it.'

A valuable and less controversial function was performed by the W.I. market stalls, of which there were about 80 in 1939 and almost 260 by early 1944, including 175 in villages. The main pre-war selling lines – eggs, poultry, cakes, butter, cream and jam – soon disappeared (although the Food Office allowed a certain amount of fat, sugar and dried fruit to 'recognised' cake makers who made cakes and buns for sale at the stalls). In their place came an increasing turnover of fruit and vegetables plus sidelines such as flowers, packets of dried herbs, chutneys, pickles, sauces and honey. The country produce associations of the W.I. and W.V.S. helped provide the villages with a steady supply of fresh food, and any surplus was directed to local factory canteens, hospitals or British restaurants.

Apart from food production and their involvement in communal feeding with such initiatives as the Rural Meat Pie Scheme, the women's organisations also assisted with evacuees, helped run rest camps, visited hospitals and worked to rehabilitate blitzed families. But they had another function, which was possibly more important than any of these: they provided a channel through which women who had taken no interest in affairs outside their homes could gain knowledge of the wider world and learn how to get things done. This was a big factor in helping women gain in self-confidence, heralding the end of the time when they were prepared simply to leave things to the men. Increasingly, women expected to have a say in both local and national administration.

Mrs Potter, a farmer's wife from Fog Close Farm at Kirkoswald in the Eden Valley in Cumberland had her first glimpse of how others lived with the arrival of evacuees:

As war broke out and the evacuation began, there came a young woman and her two children, from a city danger zone. Her husband had been on the means test three years, and she had paid 15s a week for 3 rooms! Just one more victim of these demoralising years of unemployment. She had never been in debt either. We got on well together and she opened my eyes to conditions outside my experience. After a time, as the expected bombs did not come, she drifted home again and I was left full of resentment at the social injustice of our time, and resolved to at least do my part to fight and work for better conditions for such as she.

The practical thing to do, she considered, was to join the Women's Institute:

Since the war [began] I have taken an active part in our village Women's Institute, and in the winter attend a history discussion group. In the long winter evenings, too, we knit and read. Left Book Club books, political books, autobiographies and historical novels we enjoy most.

I must confess that my family poke fun at my political enthusiasms: but I do firmly believe that we women could take a decisive part in the planning of the post-war world, and the government of it; and that we ought to be more politically minded. I certainly take more interest in politics, current affairs, and in religious work, too; and last year [1943] started a Sunday School at the village chapel, a mile away, taking the four children from here with me.

For the most capable women, the W.I. and W.V.S. could provide a career and even the means of entering into government service. Miss Edith Walker, the organiser of the fruit-preserving scheme, left the W.I. in the autumn of 1943 to go to the Ministry of Food as head of the Food Advice Division of the Ministry.

Many farmers' wives, though, were kept fully occupied running their own households under altered conditions. A Scottish woman

The Rural Meat Pie scheme in operation near Reading.

writing in *The Farmers Weekly* in August 1940 noted that after the outbreak of war:

The question arose: how were we to help and where was our help most needed? Those without ties could go forth into the active part of the fray, into any of the women's voluntary services: but countless others could not do this. After careful consideration, our decision was made. Our home and those in it had first call on our resources.

People with children and old folks in the house have their duty plain before them. There is neither sense nor reason in rushing to the aid of those in the village who are perhaps well enough served already, and leaving one's own family to the care of strangers. In an air raid a child is already frightened, but the presence of his mother is a comfort, whereas that of a stranger would make 'confusion worse confounded'.

The first [task] of course, was to see that with the foods available we should endeavour to provide sustaining and satisfying meals for the family so that work should not suffer. This meant extra planning and contriving; and the introduction of articles of food hitherto unknown or disliked by the family, but camouflaged beyond recognition, so that they asked for more.

As the danger grew nearer, we had to pack away china and fragile articles, to avoid breakages and splinters when bombs fell in the district. There were local Red Cross efforts to aid to the utmost of our ability (knitting, sewing, collecting, etc.) besides helping when required at teas and so on in connection with sales and fêtes in aid of the funds. We had to see that our old papers and periodicals were saved for the salvage campaign, not forgetting the scrap iron and metal lying about the farm.

Apart from all this the usual work of the farmer's wife had to be performed; and there arose the question of laying in extra stocks of home-made jam, jellies, pickles, bottled fruit and dried vegetables for the winter. Every inch of our garden has been devoted to the 'Dig for Victory' effort, and the results have been most gratifying.

This, then, is what the war has meant to us. Increased work, increased worry, increased expense; and also an ever increasing conviction that it will all be worth while when we see our country made safe from the invader, and Europe free from the blood-stained hands of Hitler and his henchmen.

By 1941, even the most willing of work-horses were beginning to feel the strain. The farmer's wife found herself with additional mouths to feed – evacuees, Land Girls, billeted soldiers – more rooms to clean, and more piles of washing and mending requiring attention. There was no such thing as a free Sunday. In any case, the pressures of farming were now so great that her assistance was often called for there, while if anyone fell sick it was she who would have to nurse them back to health and strength. As the call-up of women became more rigorous, she had perhaps to contend with having her daughter or any domestic servants registered for war work and posted off the farm. By the following year, there were sounds of discontent from some of those who had been lucky enough to have domestic help before the war. Their plight was even raised in Parliament in December 1942 by Mrs H.B. Tate, MP for Frome in Somerset. One suggested remedy was the formation of a Farm Indoor Staff Corps into which women would be drafted in the same way as they were directed into the services and the war factories. Another idea was the setting up of a 'house steward's branch of the W.L.A.'. This idea was vigorously denounced by the Land Girls on the grounds that such work was demeaning and not what they had signed on for, and many farmers were equally hostile to the plan. C. Stevenson from Shatwell Fold at Tytherington near Macclesfield in Cheshire asked indignantly:

Does the Government think the Land Girls are going to save the situation? All they do is add a further burden on the wretched farmer's wife, for they refuse to do anything indoors and expect to be waited on. I have had some!

In 1943 there came the belated concession from the Ministry of Labour that call-up for domestic servants could be deferred in cases of hardship. Even so, many farmers' wives continued to work as much as 15 to 18 hours a day, feeling, like Mrs Maidi Welch, that 'if only there was time for my husband or me to have a cold, and headache or bad temper, it would be a luxury.' Mrs Corrie, a farmer from Stewartry near Castle Douglas in Kirkcudbrightshire, described in *The Farmers Weekly* the evening chores she had to tackle after a full day's work seeing to the milking and feeding of her cattle, filling in forms, going to market and tackling the shopping:

The men depart to their caravan – I feed the cats, wash up and prepare broth – two gallons of it – for the next day's dinner, having 18 people to feed. As I chop up carrots, leeks, onions and kale, etc., I decide on potato soup for the day after, and lentil the day after that. The soup safely on the boil, I peel and peel potatoes; Arthur (my son) having finished lessons gives me a hand.

He goes off to bed at 9 o'clock and as the night is still young and oven good I bake two batches of oven scones and with saved rations manage a tin of gingerbread – a wartime one, of course.

I bring in anthracite, stoke up. It is now almost eleven. I make porridge for the next day and put on the kettle; I must have some tea before bed. I reach for my book, put my feet against the warm stove and have a blissful 20 minutes. The gingerbread is ready, so whisk it into the pantry, refill kettle and leave by range. Put out the

A HOME GUARD AGAINST WINTER CHILLS

lamp (how I loathe lamps, 18 years of them, always the faint aroma of paraffin about them).

In July, another farmer's wife with three children wrote to R.J. Boothby, the Conservative MP for Aberdeen East, urging him to bring the plight of others like her before the House of Commons:

I find it a physical impossibility for me, as a nursing mother, to do everything that is necessary in the way of cooking, washing, ironing, cleaning, mending, the routine of milking and keeping the utensils clean, which comprises the domestic work of a farm.

I get up at 5 o'clock in the morning and at 10 o'clock at night I still have to bath the baby, who has to be roused out of a sound sleep.

I dread to think of the harvest with all that it implies for the house-wife already over-burdened.

But when the matter was raised at Westminster, Mr McCorquodale, the Parliamentary Secretary to the Ministry of Labour could promise no further assistance. Farms, he said, had been given special priority in claims for domestic help, but the Minister had powers of persuasion only and the House would not tolerate a situation in which a person could be prosecuted, fined and possibly sent to prison for refusing to work in a private house where the defendant could not tell what the conditions would be.

And if the position for employers remained gloomy for the rest of the war, the prospects for the future were no brighter. It was clear that girls who had been in the Services would be unwilling to return to the drudgery of domestic service in peacetime. Even *Country Life* from its patrician viewpoint was aware of the stigma of inferiority attached to domestic work and opined in May 1944 that the 'servant problem would only be resolved if not only their material benefits but their status in the world's often snobbish eyes may be improved; exactly how it is to be done *is* a problem indeed.'

Much worse than the lack of domestic help for most country housewives was the difficulty of shopping for anyone who lived at all off the beaten track. As the petrol shortage restricted tradesmen's journeys, it became increasingly difficult to obtain groceries, fuel and the ordinary necessities of life. Mary Day wrote in *The Farmers Weekly* in August 1942 of a friend's experience of staying at three Scottish farmhouses – one in a Highland glen eight miles from the nearest village, one nine and the third ten miles from an East Lothian town:

All three farmers' wives had the same story to tell. Their generous hospitality could still offer plenty of vegetables, and ingenious cooking made these and the cheese ration into excellent fare.

But there was no meat. The butcher calls only once a week, and by the time he reaches the outlying places there is little left – and no choice or variety. Our farm houses are not noticeably equipped with refrigerators. A meat meal once a week sees the end of whatever the butcher has been able to let them have.

However, the meat does arrive. Everything else has to be fetched.

For all the use buses are to these remote places, there might as well not be any. The last village – wherever it may be – has always crowded them to overflowing. By the time the farmer's wife does get into the town or village, people living near the shops have bought everything up.

The odds are that the shopping expedition will end in a a nine- or ten-mile walk, with a basket heavy not with the best of war-time food, but with whatever unwanted commodity the shops have left.

When I was in Lancashire a month or two ago, up among the hills of the Lake District, everyone around there had the same problem. Women with far more than their own families to cater for – meals to prepare and pack up for men to take out to the fields, meals to have waiting for the farm workers at night – are able to get less by far than people in towns, who not only have the first chance of whatever may be in the shops, but can supplement their rations by restaurants or off-the-ration cooked food.

Canteens and pie-schemes are not a national organisation; they depend on local enterprise – and for scattered, outlying dwellings how can they operate anyway? The petrol ration would not run to it.

For many women, like Mrs Board of Home Farm, Merthymaur, near Bridgend in Glamorgan, the bicycle was the only answer.

Our farm is over two miles from the nearest small town, and as we are not fortunate enough to be on the bus route I was forced at first, when our petrol was cut down, to walk the two miles there and back, whenever I wanted to do some shopping.

Like most other farmers' wives I am doubly busy since the war, so I could afford neither the time nor the energy to do this for long. So in despair and very doubtfully, I bought a bicycle; and after a few rather painful attempts I learned to ride it. Now, I go into town on it once a week.

I am always laden down with all sorts of things. Usually there is a very dirty pair of breeches belonging to my husband to go to the cleaners, tied to the handle bars; a few pairs of shoes for the cobbler, in the basket in front; two or three library books for the family strapped to the carrier behind. My shopping bag's in my left hand; stuffed to bursting point with odds and ends such as our nine ration books and the empty orange juice and cod liver oil bottles for my small son, which must be taken to the local Food Office.

So, laden like a pedlar, I cover the two miles to town, wobbling dangerously at times, not being an expert at cycling with one hand. Coming back I am even more laden, with toothpaste, tomatoes and fish (if lucky), fresh library books, orange juice and a dozen and one other things that I have to get – from lamp glasses to fly-catchers.

In the 'old-days' – meaning before the war – shopping was a simple matter. Then, we could take the car whenever we liked, stop outside each shop and pile our purchases into the back seat. Now, it isn't even safe to leave one's cycle outside a shop unattended, too many get stolen.

For Mrs Hansard of Cater Lane farm, Thornton-le-Moor in Lincolnshire, the solution to clothing problems was mail order:

When my eldest son needed some boots, I cycled in wind and rain to the nearest town – only to find there were none his size in any shop. Next day, after a similar journey in the other direction, I did get a pair. On the whole I find shopping by post more satisfactory. One London firm supplies us in this way with most of our needs. Sometimes, though, I make a change – as when I saw a riding mackintosh advertised in *The Farmers Weekly*, and sent for it, and found it a great bargain as well as a boon. Coupons do not trouble us; I was brought up to be thrifty, and never throw anything away. When garments reach their absolute latter end, they are cut up for 'snips' and made into pegged rugs which wear as well as anything on the brick floor of a farmhouse.

Local bus services, which had provided such a lifeline to the towns for rural districts, were cut back and by September 1942 the situation was so acute in the Oban-Taynuilt District of Argyllshire that the local MP, Major McCullum, took the matter up with the Ministry of War Transport. However, nothing could be done, and country dwellers generally had to put up with enforced isolation until after the end of the war. Barbara Wilcox reflected on what it meant to be deprived of this basic means of transport in *The Farmer & Stockbreeder* in November 1944:

Three days a week the local bus passes through our village. Anxious groups gather in good time at various points, hoping that the bus will not be too full to stop. On week-days, it is ten to one that it *will* stop but a hundred to one that there won't be a seat. On Saturday morning it is ten to one that it *won't* stop and on Saturday afternoon there is no hope at all.

But until this week it was still possible to get into town by walking a mile to catch a bus on another route.

Now that last hope has been removed. The bus goes another way, and there is no means of getting to town on Saturday afternoon unless you are hardy enough to cycle ten miles there and ten back.

For four years now, shopping by the local bus has often been a nightmare journey. There is no village shop and everything must be carried back – except coal and milk, which are delivered. 'Everything', of course, includes wireless batteries, books, potatoes and other vegetables (some folks have no gardens), a month's jam and treacle ration and all personal necessities.

STRENGTHEN THE HOME FRONT

You may be fortunate enough to squeeze yourself in going to town, but you must not forget you have to get back.

This means waiting with all your parcels in a queue in the bus yard. If it is raining you get very wet, for there is no shelter. If you cannot get your own village bus, you must travel another route and walk a mile or more up hill with all your gear.

Country people are accustomed to the rough end of the stick and there has been very little complaint. Somehow or other the weekly shopping has been done and often a neighbour's too, for elderly people and mothers with young children cannot hope to go to town at all. They just stay at home.

We don't complain when the buses are filled with evacuees who have a lot more time than most of us, for, after all, they had a poor time before they came down here. And the Americans naturally want to see the town and are very polite in offering their seats, if they have one.

The bus owners do their best and try to be fair; they limit passengers to those with return tickets, giving them the first place coming back. That works well for those who could get on the bus going, but for any who struggle in some other way it is a bit hard. I have seen an elderly couple turned out into the rain because they had no return tickets.

Rural life will never be really attractive until there are reasonable facilities to get to town for shopping and recreation. It ought to be possible for all housewives to shop in moderate comfort and for working men and women to go into town on Saturday, their only afternoon off.

As things are now, country shoppers have a very poor do – they rarely have a chance of 'off the ration' food which may be available only on a day when the bus doesn't run or is sold out before the bus arrives. As for cinemas and theatres, they are hardly possible as the buses don't fit.

Many villages are more isolated and worse served than ours is. A woman I met told me that she had to walk three miles with her little boy of two and a half to catch the bus. 'He must be a very good walker,' I said. 'He's got to be,' she replied grimly.

Petrol rationing began in the last week of September 1939, before food rationing. Depending on the size of the car, the ration was enough for an average of 150 miles' motoring a month. Not surprisingly, bicycle shops began to do a roaring trade and machines that had been rusting in garages and outhouses were pressed into service. Major Jarvis remarked in *Country Life* only a fortnight or so after the start of petrol rationing that:

The shortage in petrol has brought another novel touch to our roads in village and countryside, and this is the new cyclist. Great care should be exercised when passing them for, though they may lack that desire to commit suicide which is a feature of the ordinary trained cyclist, they also lack confidence and practice, and wobble alarmingly when they hear a car behind. Until they have decided that they can ride as well as they did in the past, they are using the bicycles that the gardener and the parlourmaid lent for the occasion. On these machines one sees them proceeding slowly and gingerly, with now and then a double swerve as they did some thirty years ago in the days of Edward VII when first they learned to wobble down the lane with the cycle agent's boy trotting alongside as instructor.

Less courageous souls sought safer conveyances: horse-drawn vehicles were taken out of retirement, giving coach builders, farriers and harness makers additional work. Major Jarvis reported:

Most of the pony traps that have been lying idle for some twenty years have proved to be quite serviceable after a few repairs, and 'turn-outs' complete with pony that might have fetched £12 a month ago are now going for £30 or £40. The trouble, however, is harness, and a set that might have realised half a crown at a sale a few months ago is now worth anything from £3 to £4. That there is some profiteering going on in the harness market is not to be denied, but one must not begrudge a satisfactory turn-over to a man who had had sufficient acumen some months ago to foresee that there would be a boom in this very out-of-date commodity.

Others saw the diminishing petrol ration as a challenge. Captain C.J. Orde wrote to *Country Life* in October 1939:

Sir, – I read with interest your article in *Country Life* on petrol consumption. I own and drive a Lincoln Zephyr (twelve-cylinder, 38 hp). Since rationing of petrol came in I have managed to get about 18 mpg out of it by the following method of driving: as little choking as possible; never using the great power of acceleration; never exceeding 20 mph and coasting wherever possible, but never coasting at less than 20 mph. This is, of course, not very exciting, but I take only twenty minutes longer getting to my house in the country than I used to take when going all out. The double journey to my house in Kent – just beyond Edenbridge – is sixty-eight miles, and of that I can coast sixteen!
One soon settles down to low-speed driving, so far as I have seen I am the only one who does it. Everything on the road passes me. I have had nothing whatever done to the car. The plugs were renewed about 2,000 miles ago – the car has done 21,000 – and I see that the tyres are properly inflated. The consumption may work out at a bit over 18 mpg, so I am just about getting my 200 miles a month – C.J. Orde (Captain).
[We share Capt. Orde's impression that few motorists have yet realised the increased mileage per gallon obtainable by driving at a lower speed, as our Motoring Correspondent explained in a recent article. – Ed.]

By early 1940, many motorists decided that it was no longer worth keeping their vehicles licensed. The number of licences issued dropped from 2.3 million the previous August to about 1.4 million by the end of March. The inveterate driver, however, was not so easily put off, and substitutes for petrol were investigated. The Honourable Maynard Greville advised enthusiasts in January 1940 to try using producer gas, either relying entirely on the gas, or retaining the petrol carburettor so that the car could be started from cold on petrol before switching over to gas after a few minutes running. Gas did have its disadvantages: apart from the rather peculiar appearance of the car, there was definite loss of performance – a certain amount of pinking was inevitable – and dealing with stops was awkward. But with skilful handling the petrol/gas car could do something like 100 miles to the gallon.

Motorists still using their cars in the summer of 1940 could have some difficulty in finding their way in unfamiliar territory. Not only had the signposts been uprooted to confuse the enemy in the event of invasion, but strangers asking directions of the local inhabitants were liable to be suspected of being spies.

The blackout, too, continued to pose a hazard for pedestrians and other road users, with some 8,600 deaths and perhaps a quarter of a million casualties during the course of 1940. Most accidents occurred on open country roads, rather than in the towns where a 20 mph speed limit kept the carnage in check. The chief cause of accidents seems to have been reckless driving by army vehicles, and the War Office did not admit any liability to compensate civilian casualties. With the increase in military traffic and, in particular, the coming of American convoys later in the war, the toll rose still further. *Country Life* in March 1941 advised pedestrians to wear white spats to ensure they were seen, a sartorial adjustment that few countrymen will have made.

The production of new cars for civilian use ceased in November 1940, and the 400 new cars in the hands of manufacturers and dealers at the time were ordered to be allocated to doctors in rural areas, to inspectors of aircraft production and the police in cases where it could be shown that secondhand models were not readily available. Curiously, though, manufacturers continued to advertise their products throughout the war, presumably to make sure that demand remained afterwards.

The petrol ration was cut in the autumn of 1941 and again in the spring of 1942 as merchant shipping losses cut back the supply of crude oil at the same time as the requirements of the forces – particularly the RAF – were rising sharply. Petrol coupons were like gold dust, although the odd gallon or two could sometimes be cadged from a sympathetic garage owner. At about this time, the author's parents drove from Plymouth to Rosyth in Scotland with only sufficient coupons for the outward journey. Their return was aided by one proprietor, 'a little Scottish woman in a bobble hat', who willingly filled the tank while fulminating against the government that was ruining her business. 'To hell with them, when it's gone it's gone.' Any chance of such adventures came to an end when the petrol ration for private motorists was withdrawn altogether on 1st July 1942.

Farmers were better placed, as they could claim special allowances of fuel for tractors, stationary engines and vans and lorries operating on an F licence. Not that the ration was generous: only with the strictest economy was enough left for the demands of the harvest and autumn ploughing. Farmers' private cars and lorries operating on carrier's licences were excluded, even if they were used for marketing. Mr M.B. Warren of Abbots Inn, Crowthorne, Berkshire protested in *The Farmer & Stock-breeder* in March 1944:

I think the least I am entitled to is to be allowed enough petrol to run my car twice a week to the nearest town – five miles away – to supply two markets and two greengrocers, as I did last year, which entailed the necessity of hiring a car and trailer.

I am denied any at all and have had to reply that there is no alternative other than to let my crops decay when they are ready for consumption and delivery.

The obvious temptation for farmers entitled to special allowances was to apply for more than they required so that they could have a gallon or two for private purposes – the luckiest were those with their own storage tanks. Even then, the trick was to have a business reason for any journey, just in case you were stopped and interrogated by the law. Mrs Blackmore recalls:

On the whole we were all fairly honest and caring about wartime supplies. For instance our tractors then used TVO but had to be started on petrol, so when we put in for our extra ration of petrol we asked for a little more than absolutely necessary – the amount was usually reduced but we gained a little. Our market town was 15 to 20 miles away, and we were allowed petrol for church, but when rationing became very severe and we were supposed to be able to justify our journeys we took a sack of potatoes or apples to our greengrocer in a seaside town five miles away, so that we could visit our friends or go to the cinema or a dance.

Even shorter or more necessary excursions carried a risk of prosecution. In January 1943, 22 Cumberland farmers appeared before magistrates on charges arising out of two funerals – one of a farmer at Plumpton, near Penrith and the other of a farmer's son at Kirkoswald. Some of the defendants were relatives of the deceased and some were neighbours acting as bearers at the funerals. 'I think it is most regrettable,' said the defence solicitor, 'that, in order to gain publicity for these cases (as a warning to others), the authorities have considered it necessary to send policemen to funerals.' Nevertheless nineteen were fined between 5s. and 20s. and only three cases were dismissed.

Petrol rationing put such treats as a cinema out of reach for anyone who lived outside the towns. Mrs Board from Glamorgan told *The Farmers Weekly* that 'in winter cycling two miles there and back in freezing darkness – our fingers numb around the handle-bars and the wind pressing us so it seems we are not moving at all – well even Tyrone Power isn't worth it.' The difficulty in getting to town entertainments produced a revival of home-grown recreation. An Oxford villager told *The Farmers Weekly* in October 1944:

The war has undoubtedly altered our way of living considerably. The village has come to life again, since it has become so difficult to get to our nearest town, 6 miles away. During the winter we have whist drives – everyone makes an effort to go to them all – and they are really like a big family gathering . . . And, of course, there are auctions, jumble sales and teas in aid of this and that. All this means that we really know and enjoy our own community – as we did not, when transport was easier.

Mrs Blackmore remembers the local dances and hunt balls, mostly in aid of the Red Cross:

They were fantastic occasions under the circumstances – many of the committee members were of the farming community and they pulled out 'all the stops' . . . Needless to say, civilians and servicemen of all nationalities packed out village halls and ballrooms – and once the servicemen found a farmer's daughter to dance with – one could see them thinking 'food, eggs, cream and butter' before consideration of 'charm, figure or looks'. I had a good test to see if they wanted to take me home, it was at least five miles each way, five farm gates one way and three farm gates and a muddy lane at the other – that sorted them out. Often my evening dress was in the saddle bag of my bicycle, if I didn't feel the Red Cross justified the use of petrol.

In some places, the village pub remained as crowded as ever. The young men might have left, but there were now passing lorry drivers, servicemen and itinerant officials coming in with news of how Coventry or Cardiff were taking it, or where a special consignment of off-the-ration goods might be bound. The older habitués could find themselves dragged out of dark corners by intruders who wanted a darts game or have their sense of propriety offended by the presence of young women, perhaps being taken to a country inn for the first time by soldier boy-friends.

Many of the older country people, though, preferred to stay at home in the evenings and listen to the radio, providing the near-unobtainable batteries held out. Mrs Sutherland of Sibster Farm at Halkirk in Caithness wrote to *The Farmers Weekly* in October 1944:

The wireless, which was really little used in peacetime, is now one of our most precious possessions, so many from here have gone to war that the news of the progress of the various battle fronts is listened to with breathless interest; and almost all our social activities are connected with some branch of war works. We used to play rather a lot of whist of an evening, especially in the long winter evenings, but I have scarcely handled cards since 1939.

The nine o'clock news was usually a must, especially where a husband or son was serving overseas, although not all listeners considered that the BBC's treatment of the war gave suffient attention to deeds of gallantry. *The Field* looked at broadcasting in August 1942:

In these matters it isn't easy to discriminate between the BBC and the Ministry of Information for they are of the Box and Cox order. Analysis of a recent broadcast showed that from five to six minutes was sufficient for the war in Russia and Egypt and three more for various world affairs. The rest of 23 minutes was devoted to pensions, bakers' wages, coal mining, welfare of war workers and a speech in the Lords dealing with finance after the war, the gold standard, the assurance that no tragic errors would be repeated, and much more concerning the Winning of the Peace. Three citations of the gallant deeds our men were doing to help to Win the War were judged worthy to come at the end of this miscellany.

The wireless as a power for propaganda is unrivalled; it can either inspire a nation or sap its vitality, and the crooning, drooling and meaningless drivel that has been poured out can only have had a deleterious effect on the morality of the younger generation. Its psychological effect is to produce a paralysis of mind only rivalled by that created by the glamour film importations. A sense of proportion is lost and a lack of stability results which makes itself felt in every serious endeavour.

The radio was an important means of conveying information to farmers. At the start of war, the BBC already had a good reputation with rural listeners, thanks largely to John Green, the BBC's farming expert, who had his own holding in the Cotswolds and knew the mind of the farming community. It was his job during the war to see that farming talks fitted in with government policy, which he managed without any heavy-handed ministerial interference. One wartime

The FARMERS WEEKLY

4d

VOL. XVI. No. 13 [REGISTERED AT THE G.P.O. AS A NEWSPAPER]   FRIDAY, MARCH 27, 1942   FOURPENCE WEEKLY

Issued by the National Compound Cattle Food Manufacturers

Save ships, Mr. Farmer!

If every appeal was as easy to meet as this one there'd not be much grumbling.

It goes this way. Much of the essential food required for milk production has to come from abroad.

If you use every ounce of feeding stuffs as efficiently and as economically as possible, you will be saving valuable shipping space and the lives of the men of our Merchant Navy.

How to do it? Use National Compounds. They reduce labour and increase your profits. But, more important still, they make strict rationing easy—and that means less ships needed.

Moreover, all cattle like them . . . and you know what that means.

IMPORTANT

National Cattle Food No. 1 *is a complete milk production ration, not to be "unbalanced" by adding corn. If users find that they have surplus Protein coupons left after buying their Dairy Cake, they should use these to buy National High Protein Concentrate, which needs Protein coupons only, or 'Grain Balancer which needs 1 Protein : 1 Cereal.*

Compounds ease convoys

venture, started in April 1942, was *Country Magazine*, a radio show that was compered first by A.G. Street and then by Ralph Wightman. As Street later wrote:

The fighting services, ARP, munitions, and townsfolk generally were well catered for; but somehow country people and their war-work

175

were not getting their rightful share of publicity. There were plenty of music hall jokes about fatstock prices, possibly too many technical talks on farming practice; but something more was needed. Could there be a programme that would tell soldier, sailor, airman and town dweller just what was happening in the countryside? In short, could British broadcasting show the nation and the world that half the battle of the Atlantic was being fought and won on the fields of Britain?

The programme went out every other Sunday immediately after the one o'clock news; its signature tune, 'The Painful Plough', accompanied the mid-day meal in thousands of homes across the country. It was an instant success, because, as Street wrote,

. . . the farmer, the farm worker, the butcher, the baker, the cobbler, the saddler, the huntsman, the squire, the doctor, the retired colonel, the vet, the Home Guard, Uncle Tom Cobley and all, together with their womenfolk, could and did rub shoulders in the studio and broadcast, not what the producer might want them to say, but what they themselves wanted to say. There was never the slightest suggestion of importing a countryman to London to put him on a pin and let him wriggle in front the microphone for the amusement of town listeners.

Much more than before the war, country people relied on newspapers to keep them in touch with the outside world. Mrs Sutherland in remote Caithness remarked that 'the papers – so much shrunk since the war – are really *read* by everyone.' In addition to a daily and perhaps a local paper, most farm families took either *The Farmers Weekly* or *The Farmer & Stock-breeder* on subscription. Both were high-quality publications with well respected editors. R.W. Haddon of *The Farmer & Stock-breeder* chaired the Government's Advisory Committee on Publicity for the farming industry, and it was he who spotted the slogan Dig for Victory in a leading article in the London *Evening Standard* written by Michael Foot. Haddon was also Chairman of the Red Cross Agricultural Fund, which raised £8.5 million during the course of the war. Malcolm Messer at *The Farmers Weekly* led an equally capable team, and both papers played a valuable role both in getting across the Government's Agricultural Policy and in advising farmers on the best scientific practice. *Country Life* and *The Field* also ran throughout the war, albeit on less glossy paper than before and with a more serious tone – space was devoted to the question of postwar construction as well as to familiar country house topics.

The curtailment of sport during the war was heralded by the cutting short of one of the best cricket seasons for years at the beginning of September 1939, by which time Yorkshire had already secured the championship and the West Indies had left for home. Football was reduced largely to charity matches between service elevens and professional players, while hunting and racing were scarcely to be thought of. Indeed, some hunts responded to the outbreak of war by destroying their hounds. Blankney in Lincolnshire had put down ten couples by the end of September 1939, leaving 35 couples for the control of foxes. The Master was quoted as saying that if the war lasted for any time, more would have to be destroyed, and if the foxes remained troublesome they would have to be shot.

By the end of the year, some sports were reviving. In October, the Masters of Foxhounds Association sent a circular to its members pointing out how prejudicial it would be to the country in general if hunting were allowed to lapse altogether: 'it should be kept on as long as conditions permitted to exterminate foxes, to keep packs going and to provide 'officers on leave with a much needed solace.' With staffs already depleted by the calling up of men, many of those who cheered hounds into coverts were now women, who were also taking over the organisation of the packs. Some hunts were hit by the buying up of remounts for the army. Although the regular cavalry had been reduced to three regiments, there were still a number of Yeomanry Regiments to be horsed. With the effects of rationing on forage and hound food, it was expected that packs would be able to operate at roughly half strength. The opening meet at Croome was a meagre affair compared with previous years, as its secretary lamented in *The Field* in November 1939:

Where is the pomp and splendour of brave scarlet and gleaming topper? The rows of horse boxes, the general 'spit and polish' (if you will permit the expression) of the first day of the season proper? Instead we find sober black coats and ratcatchers interspersed with khaki; unclipped horses and a sadly depleted field.

By the opening of the following year's season, more than 3,000 couples of hounds had been destroyed and the fodder shortage was acute. There were critics who wondered whether 'with Hitler's fists at the gate and clamouring to get in', hunting should not be stopped altogether, but the hunt correspondent of *The Field* was anxious to point out that the sport had military advantages, for 'quite apart from the exercise, the troops will have the grandest opportunity in the world to sharpen their observational faculties and to learn to find their way about in unfamiliar country districts.' Whether following the hounds on foot or horseback, the townsperson in uniform

. . . will soon acquire that automatic habit which is one of the attributes of the hunting man; that is to look for and see as soon as he gets into a field the way to get out of it on any of the other three sides. He will learn to notice the lie of the land, to see at once the point of vantage where he can survey the surrounding country and to spot cover where he can conceal himself so that he can see the fox and not be seen. Indeed, if he can hide from the cunning eyes and nose of a fox he should have no difficulty in coping with a German on land or in the air.

Such special pleading proved unnecessary, and hunting, patronised by many a squire among the high command and by leading farmers on the War Ags, managed to survive the war. Masters, though, had to adapt their fixture lists to ensure that no damage was done to plough land in spring, and by 1942 the fodder situation had deteriorated so far that it only allowed the 'maintenance of 314 horses in hunt establishments throughout England and Wales.' The secretary of the Hampshire hunt told a reporter early that year, 'there is no hunting for amusement nowadays. We only hunt to kill foxes and in our case we are stopping at the end of February.' With hunting in eclipse, the fox population increased. In February 1943, the Cumberland War Ag organised a drive over fells once hunted by John Peel to eliminate local foxes which were taking the Herdwick ewes, and at the same time in Perthshire, the farmers of the Dunning and Auchterarder district rallied 60 guns and 200 military beaters to clear foxes from Craig Rossie in what was claimed to be the largest fox hunt ever to have taken place in the county.

Some racehorse owners took precipitate action before anything definite was known about the outlook for racing. The outstanding prospect for the 2,000 guineas, the colt Rose of England was taken out of training in September 1939, as were a number of other leading contenders. Many meetings were abandoned, including the Champagne Stakes at Doncaster and the Middle Park Stakes at

Newmarket, both key races for showing the merit of two-year-olds. By the end of October, however, nerves had steadied and racing had resumed, largely to maintain the stables and the profitable bloodstock business. The flat-racing season also started well in spite of misgivings about continuing as the news from France became worse. Even *Country Life* had reservations about racing results being broadcast at the end of the news.

It is certainly curious to hear the results of race meetings announced on the News following immediately on the nightly tidings of the life and death struggle in France. Reactions to it are bound to be mixed. To some, to whom we may suspect the Turf is never a prime interest, it is abhorrent that Allied nationals should be given the impression that in this country the winning of a race is reckoned as vital as a battle – as indeed it would be were not this reasoning based on complete misunderstanding. To others the change from war to sport brings a needful relaxation of almost intolerable tension. On the whole, it is probably a psychological mistake to include racing news in the National bulletins.

On 18th June 1940, racing was suspended, largely because of the heavy burden that meetings placed on the police and defence forces generally, and continuing was felt to be inappropriate at such critical times. Racing was seen by its detractors as a costly amusement quite out of touch with the feelings of the ordinary man in time of war. Why, they asked, should labour, money and petrol be expended for no very good reason at a time when everybody was urged to save and concentrate to the utmost on the war effort.

Yet only a couple of months later the government changed its mind and racing resumed on 14th September. The chief argument in favour of continuing was the need to test bloodstock, which was an important export, and in any case, racing provided a welcome diversion for the people who enjoyed it. Nevertheless, it was to be confined to the available courses and kept to a small scale. New restrictions announced by the Home Secretary in March 1942 limited racing to Stockton and Pontefract for horses training north of the Trent, and Windsor and Salisbury for those in the south. The other course that remained open was Newmarket, which was to be the meeting place for horses aspiring to classic honours. Defending his decision not to prohibit the sport altogether, Mr Morrison declared that the government's aim was 'not to make total war, total misery.'

Although Lords remained opened as the epitome of cricket and of the national character during the emergency, the sport in wartime was reduced to scratch matches with teams drawn from the services, clubs, private elevens and government departments. On the village green on Saturday afternoons, deadly confrontations continued, although they might now be between a Home Guard eleven and a team from the local military camp. The Canadians and particularly the American troops added a new dimension to rural sport as they were wont to invite the locals to take them on at baseball or even American football. The outcome of such encounters was usually a foregone conclusion, although Tadworth Home Guard in Surrey is recorded as having put up a magnificent performance at baseball against the Canadian Highlanders in November 1940 before bowing to superior force. The honour of the home team was usually recovered on the football pitch, the complex rules of cricket being sufficient to deter most North Americans from attempting the game.

Servicemen from overseas usually spent their leave equipped with maps and gazetteers touring Britain's beauty spots, and the almost deserted roads meant that they saw the countryside at its best. The peace and quiet was also welcome therapy for ramblers and cyclists taking a few hours or days away from the hell of the blitzed cities to recharge their energies by drinking in the wildness of the Peak or Lake Districts or the civilised calm of the Cotswolds. Caravanning enjoyed a surprising revival, largely because most country cottages were being used for evacuees or as weekend haunts for the well-off. At the beginning of war, there was no demand for caravans, which were mainly sold at rock-bottom prices for use as Home Guard observation posts. But in April 1941, *Country Life* reported that

. . . a veritable boom has set in and not a van is unsold. In normal times the caravan dealer could be certain of letting his vans only for the two holiday months. Today practically all his stock-in-trade is hired already and is likely to remain so for the duration of the war.

A caravan or cottage in some remote place was partly a safe haven but also gave access to a green and pleasant land where the war could seem transient and shadowy, and nature the abiding reality. One Londoner wrote to *The Farmers Weekly* in September 1944:

I am as reluctant to leave the country as I was to leave London. It is with deep regret that I shall say good-bye to these beautiful windy upland fields where, with the plover crying and the sun shining on the ripening corn, I have found much refreshment of spirit. I have recovered my sanity in a part of England where the insanity of war has not to any extent penetrated.

Despite all its horrors and miseries, war did have a credit side. At least for the time being, the countryman came into his own, and the drift to the towns was stemmed. Once those who could be spared (and some who could not) had gone into the Armed Forces, country people settled down to fight the war in their own way with commendable unity of purpose. Church and Chapel, farmer and farm worker, women and children all pulled together perhaps as never before, in a combined effort to work, save and to pray for victory. The countryside once again looked cared for, the fields were highly productive, and the land was playing its part in feeding the nation. Morale in the villages had improved, old properties were done up, rural industries had a new burst of vigour, and communities again had a full and lively life.

But what would happen when the war was over? After all, much of the old social hierarchy of the countryside remained, and there were still only too many reminders of the way that the ownership and control of land maintained the division between rich and poor, between the leisured and the labouring classes. In his book *English Fox Hunting* Raymond Carr recalls one significant wartime incident:

Lord Leconfield, hunting in the winter of 1940 with only his whipper in and his heir, rode towards what he thought was a halloa only to find himself at a village football match. He stood up in his stirrups and shouted 'Haven't you people got anything better to do in wartime than to play football?' Then he went on hunting.

There were of course more enlightened land owners: Sir Richard Acland advocated the nationalisation of land and made over the greater part of his estates in Devon to the National Trust as an example. Because his action was based on personal morality, it was likely to be viewed as cranky, but economic pressures were soon to force many landed families to sell up or follow suit. The servant problem indicated a shift in outlook among working people: after the war they would be less tolerant of ideas of social rank and more determined to have a decent wage, a comfortable home and better public services. The farmer's wife might be appalled by the poverty of the East End evacuees but the labourer's spouse was envious

when she heard at first hand of the convenience of a gas oven, piped water and an indoor lavatory. American values, too, had their impact on country people who were struck by the indifference to authority, the relentless determination to get ahead and the joy of owning such desirable gadgetry as ice boxes, vacuum cleaners and washing machines. Although the wave of urban and foreign visitors was to recede, the effect on rural expectations was irrevocable. D.H. Lawrence commented, 'Even the farm labourer today is psychologically a town bird.'

Broadcasting to town and country alike, the BBC helped diminish the differences between them. Demobbed servicemen were determined that the old class relationships had had their day and that things were going to be different in the post-war world. The landed classes might still, in the main, vote Conservative, but the rural have-nots joined their urban brethren to help in bringing about the Labour landslide of 1945. It remained to be seen how far the new government would be able to put into effect its plans for rural reconstruction in the face of enormous economic difficulties.

Ploughing with a horse team in the Lake District, 1940.

180

Chapter 6
VICTORY AND AFTER

The last black-out restrictions were lifted on 20th April 1945, just in time for the VE Day celebrations which followed the final capitulation of Germany on 8th May. Although some commercial uses of electric lighting were still banned because of the coal shortage, the night of 8th May was illuminated by the ruddy glow of thousands of bonfires lit up and down the country. The most exuberant celebrations happened in London and the other blitzed cities where street parties and neighbourhood knees-ups went on for days. But the countryside, too, rejoiced: bunting and flags were hung out, lavish teas were organised on village greens, toasts were drunk to victory in many a local pub and churches everywhere were filled with people giving thanks for a safe deliverance. Later, when there was more time, parades were organised through the market towns, with Land Girls marching in uniformed ranks, forks and spades on their shoulders and convoys of farm machinery behind, to remind the population at large that the land had also played its part.

The festivities were underlaid by a feeling of exhaustion. A.G. Street wrote on VE Day that there would be 'celebrations, bonfires,

Passing the saluting base for the Victory Parade in the Mall are two trailer lorries bearing a land drainage excavator and a Women's Land Army tractor.

Prisoners of war at work on a clamp of potatoes at Swanley in Kent in February 1947.

public holidays and all the rest; but I think most middle-aged people, especially farming folk, will be too tired to bother with them.'

Farmers were apprehensive that there could be a repeat of the 'great betrayal' of 1921, when the state abandoned its policy of support. But this time, with world food shortages causing prices to rise and making imports expensive at a point when Britain was faced with a serious balance of payments problem, they need not have worried. The state was committed to the growth and increasing self-sufficiency of British agriculture, and the principle of support was formalised in the Agriculture Act passed by the Labour Government in 1947, which gave farmers guaranteed prices and markets for as much meat, cereals, potatoes and sugar beet as they could produce. Less popular with the farmers was the retention of the wartime disciplinary powers of enforced supervision and ultimately dispossession; more than 3,000 supervision orders were issued and over 150 farmers were dispossessed between March 1948 and the discontinuation of these measures at the end of 1951.

That such powers were thought necessary was an indication of just how serious the food shortage was in the immediate post-war years. In 1946, bread, cakes, flour and oatmeal were rationed, which they had not been at any time during the war. Even though bread rationing was intended only as a temporary measure, it lasted two years. With the termination of Lend-Lease in the early autumn of 1945, such established favourites as American canned meat and fish disappeared from the British diet. Their replacements, purchased on the world market by the Ministry of Food, were often a lot less palatable – among the most notorious was a South African canned fish unglamorously named Snoek. The new Minister of Food, John Strachey, was a less adept salesman than Lord Woolton, and his ministry had lost much of its flair as the brightest staff had returned to their pre-war occupations. The public, which had been willing to make sacrifices during the war now became increasingly impatient at being faced in peacetime with an even more austere diet.

Things got worse before they got better with the ferocious winter of 1947-48 devastating the potato crop and forcing the government to introduce controlled distribution to give each customer 3 lb per week. Milk, too, was in short supply.

It was not until 1950 that the situation improved conspicuously, allowing most of the remaining wartime controls to be dismantled

German prisoners of war clear the snow off the railway line near Hadfield in Derbyshire in February 1947.

by the Conservative government which came to power in 1951. The new administration was keen to curtail state intervention in agriculture, although it remained firmly wedded to the principle of state support.

Most farmers were aware that change was coming to agriculture and that they would require more capital to adapt to altered circumstances. The day of the small man who just turned over a few pounds for the maintenance of his family and farm was over; dog and stick husbandry would no longer do. Even a dairy farmer with only a few cows had to cull out his TB animals and consider putting in a concrete floor to upgrade his buildings. A new insistence on food hygiene and quality also meant that the whole structure of marketing would have to be revised. The future would require better educated farmers, and it was noticeable that more sons and daughters of farmers were being sent to agricultural college. This in turn led to an improvement in the social status of farmers; as one commentator put it 'from being near the bottom of the pile they rose to being pretty near the top.'

The 1950s brought increasing prosperity for British farmers, although the small hill farmers remained vulnerable. The cereal barons, on the other hand could hardly fail to coin money. This was not entirely because of price guarantees and subsidies but because of a fundamental shift in the economic equations of farming that had not been anticipated at the end of the war. The worry then had been that the disappearance of the wartime labour force of Land Girls and prisoners of war would leave the land with a serious shortage of labour. The factor that had been underestimated was the relative lowering of farmers' costs: in the 1950s and 1960s, the biological revolution in farming allowed output to be boosted with ever-increasing quantities of moderately inexpensive agricultural chemicals, while mechanisation dealt with the scarcity and increasing costs of labour by replacing men with machines.

Farmers from Canada gather round a British potato-planting machine at Shillingford in Oxfordshire. Helping to operate it are three prisoners of war.

The Queen inspects 500 members of the Women's Land Army at Buckingham Palace on 21st October 1950 as a final ceremony before the disbanding of the W.L.A. at the end of the following month.

Land Girls putting on protective clothing before using hand sprays to control pests in orchards at Colwall in Herefordshire in February 1948. Barrier creams had been found to offer insufficient protection to the skin from the effects of the sprays.

During and just after the war, though, attempts had been made to prevent people leaving the land by raising wages. The national minimum farm wage went from 48s in July 1940 to 60s in December 1943 and to 70s in March 1945. By 1950, farm wages stood at about £5 for a 47 hour week. Holidays with pay were introduced, albeit on a less than generous scale: from May 1944, agricultural workers in England and Wales were entitled to six days' holiday a year, with an extra day off for those regularly employed on Sundays. But the wartime government also realised that improved pay alone was not going to halt the drift from the land. The Scott Report, published in 1942, urged the provision of 50,000 new cottages, laid-on water and power supplies, more village halls and playing fields and better rural schools. Housing was seen as particularly appalling. According to one observer, many rural homes were characterised by 'damp walls, rough brick floors, fire-eating cookers, sculleries with sinks that were so old and worn that nobody could keep them clean or with no sinks

at all, kitchens without cupboards or drying space and no bigger than passages, neck-breaking stairs and tiny bedrooms.' As early as February 1943, rural district councils were empowered to provide 3,000 new cottages before the coming harvest. Each was to have three bedrooms, a bathroom and suitable outbuildings, and the rent was not to exceed 10s a week plus rates. A year later, less than 300 cottages had been built, and these often lacked modern fittings.

The traditional form of housing for farm workers, the tied cottage, still survived and indeed flourished in the post-war years. The custom of a low-rent cottage going with a low-paid job was defended by the farmers as being essential where the worker needed to be on immediate call (as in caring for livestock) and as a considerable perk. The farm workers' union, the N.U.A.A.W., on the other hand, saw tied housing as a way of holding down wages and inhibiting mobility, as a man might be forced to put up with a bad employer if the alternative was for him and his family to be turned out of their home at short notice. Despite the union's efforts, the tied cottage system actually grew in importance as pressure on rural housing increased: Howard Newby has estimated that between 1948 and 1976 the proportion of farm workers living in tied accommodation increased from perhaps a third to over half.

In other ways, rural standards of living did improve after the war. After the electricity industry was nationalised in 1947, the supply network was extended in the countryside, and by 1950 electricity was said to be available to four-fifths of rural homes, with only the smallest or almost remote hamlets not yet connected. The laying of water pipes and main sewerage, another immense undertaking, was needed to lift rural water supplies from their pre-war state of total inadequacy. A White Paper published in 1944 estimated that up to thirty per cent of the rural population of England and Wales had no main supplies. Many villages had to rely on standpipes, which froze in winter, or on water carts. Earth, bucket and chemical closets were still common and horror stories about health risks abounded. It was reported that in one village near Daventry in Northamptonshire the water, which was delivered three times a week, was put in dustbins from which householders drew their supply. At Keevil in Wiltshire, five farms took their drinking water from a brook into which ran all the drainage from the farms, and from which the cattle drank, inevitably leaving their dung behind them. The White Paper proposed spending £21 million to help bring piped water and better sanitation to 'almost every village, farm and cottage over the next five to seven years.'

The quality of education, too, urgently needed improving in rural areas. The 1944 Education Act had resulted in the majority of country children over the age of 11 having to attend a school outside their own village. With a secondary school curriculum that was now national in scope, rural children became assimilated into a mass culture and many grew intolerant of the social and cultural dullness of village life with its parochial view of the world. They became aware of the low status of farm workers outside their own rural areas and preferred to look for employment in the towns.

The drift from the land, temporarily halted during the war, resumed in the post-war years. In the 1950s, about 150,000 full-time workers left the industry, representing an annual loss of about three per cent. Unlike the farmers, they had failed, as their Union's president, Edwin Gooch, put it, 'to find their place in the sun'. Moreover, as the gap between their wages and those of unskilled industrial workers widened, the pull of the towns became even more irresistible. Life in the countryside may no longer have been 'dark, muddy and boring', as George Bernard Shaw once put it, but the depopulated

Jean Gibbon, a civil servant from Rutherglen in Glasgow, one of a group of 80 volunteer harvest workers spending a working holiday in Perthshire in August 1948.

villages, particularly in the north and west of the country, told their own story of declining hopes and opportunities. Ironically enough, as some rural areas were losing their population, others were gaining new inhabitants, with more and more people moving away from the noisy, grimy and congested city centres. The growing separation of homes and work places, which had begun in the 1930s, brought with it suburbanisation, ribbon development and the growth of commuter towns and villages, especially in the south east. The threat to the countryside led to a demand for rigorous planning controls, which was not met until 1947 when the Labour government's Town and Country Planning Act effectively nationalised development rights in land. Henceforward no new building could take place without planning permission from the County Council or County Borough Council. The big weakness of the Act was that much agricultural development and afforestation were exempt from control, so that it did not greatly influence changes in the farmed landscape.

The 1940s and 1950s saw the extension of Green Belts, which stopped the cities spilling further into the countryside, and the initiation of the New Towns programme to decant city dwellers into totally planned settlements with adequate services, which it was hoped would relieve pressure on the villages and, by adroit selection of sites, on the richer agricultural areas.

The need for measures to deal with the impact on the countryside of increased leisure time and the expansion of car ownership had been anticipated as early as the 1920s, with the Council for the Preservation of Rural England spearheading the National Parks movement in the '30s. But it was not until 1949 that the first National Parks legislation was enacted, with the aim of conserving areas of beautiful and relatively untamed countryside and making them available for public enjoyment.

However, the impact of waves of leisure-seekers from towns on the face of rural Britain was as nothing to that of modern commercial farming. With agriculture largely excluded from the 1947 Town and Country Planning Act and its development positively stimulated by the Agriculture Act of the same year, it was assumed that farmers would act as good stewards of the countryside. Price support was going to ensure that the dereliction of the '30s would give way to a well-husbanded and harmonious landscape that was aesthetically pleasing as well as economically prosperous. Modern farming methods were welcomed in areas of the national parks where they were thought to be appropriate – run-down farm land would be brought back into productive use, leaving nature raw and triumphant only in the higher, wilder places.

By the 1960s, the new approaches to farming that had gained impetus during World War II were giving cause for alarm. All over lowland Britain, hedges were being grubbed out to make easier working for new and more powerful machines; ponds were filled in, copses and woodland areas reduced or removed. Elsewhere, heath, moorland and wetlands came under attack as the boundaries of cultivation were relentlessly extended. In the face of high cereal prices, downland sheepwalks, herb-rich meadows, reedy fens and valley mires fell victim to the plough.

It is now possible to see all this as merely a continuation of a long term trend towards the intensification of agriculture, resulting in the loss of landscape diversity, specialised habitats and previously abundant wildlife. Arguably, farming had been progressing in this direction since the Agricultural Revolution of the mid 17th century, interrupted only by the great depressions of the late 19th century and the years between the two World Wars. What has altered since World War II has been the pace of change – those years of striving for productivity during the war constituted a watershed for the British countryside, after which nothing could be quite the same again. More than thirty years later, it is only too easy to see how high the cost has been. The Government has seen agriculture as its 'green oil', but the wealth of farmers and of the farming industry (at least until the 1980s) has been purchased at the expense of empty fields and an increasingly monotonous and dehumanised landscape. How ironic it is that this countryside, environmentally impoverished where before the war it was financially depressed, and now deserted by so many of its own people, is expected to provide refreshment and revitalisation for visitors from the towns.